LACE
VILLAGES

LACE
VILLAGES

B. T. Batsford Ltd London

Dedication

This book is dedicated to my family past and present, but especially to my parents, Don and Terry Caesar, my god-parents, Joyce Caesar, Ken Brown and Paddy Bellett and to my Aunt Mary and Uncle Alan.

ISBN 0 7134 9813 2

A catalogue record for this book is available from the British Library

Typeset by Goodfellow & Egan Ltd., Cambridge and printed in Great Britain by Courier International, East Kilbride, Scotland for the Publisher
B.T. Batsford Ltd
4 Fitzhardinge Street
London W1H 0AH

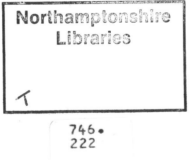

CONTENTS

FOREWORD

When I had written the number of words that I was expected to write, I felt that I had exhausted all I could say on the subject, only to discover that I had barely touched the tip of the iceberg. Thousands of places are out there to visit and many more stories exist, some from villages that I had not previously associated with lacemaking. I was fortunate to find many people in the less well-known villages who were happy to recall for me the time of the lace trade; a fascinating picture began to emerge. People have been most generous with time, memory, and documentary evidence to support my research and so I have spent the last few months agonizing over the stories and information that I could not include. In the end I came to the conclusion that there is so much to say about the clever, brave and sometimes comical inhabitants of the 'Lace Villages', and of lacemakers past and present, that I could take a lifetime and still not say it all.

Patterns have been a major problem; I have been inundated with them. Unfortunately, many that I might have used, on close examination were too inaccurate. I hope that you will enjoy those included: wherever possible I have given some reference to where I obtained them, and explained their relevance to the section in which they are included.

I make Bucks Point, and so I have been able to offer some Point Ground designs trued and re-worked, albeit in my own fashion, which you may or may not agree with. The Bedford patterns I have included for your interest, untrued and, except in one case, untried. I am not sure of the accuracy of the prickings, although I have taken the repeats from obviously undamaged areas, and I offer them to you 'just as they came out of Granny's attic'. I hope that they are of interest and I shall look forward to lacemakers showing me the results.

Liz Bartlett

ACKNOWLEDGEMENTS

I would like to thank all those who unreservedly gave time and memories, loaned lace equipment, and offered help and advice in the preparation of this work. Special thanks go to Jack, Kathy and Tricia Roper, Mary Harrison, Ivy Clarke, and the late Clara Webb and her family, all of whom assisted greatly in the gathering of information and in the 'trial runs'. For advice, research and permission to use extracts from her late husband's invaluable work may I thank Lady Frances Markham. For hours of putting up with my grumbles and for her research work on the Bedfordshire villages, love and thanks to Pat Janes of Chiltern Lacemakers.

Many thanks to Sylvia Bull and the Trustees of the Cowper and Newton Museum, Iris Martin, Maggie Nevitt and Roger Kitchen, and all those concerned with the Living Archive Project. I would like to thank Bernard Cavalot, who tirelessly found references in obscure antiquarian books and papers that gave me entirely new perspectives on Stony Stratford. For introducing me to the world of old books, and thus single-handedly contributing more to the penury of the Bartlett household than any one person before – Bernard, my thanks!

I have met so many people in the course of pursuing information about the Lace Villages that it would be impossible for me to acknowledge everybody whose contribution (greatly disparaged by themselves) allowed me to complete the work. Many thanks to John Mercer, whose quick brain and deft hand thought out the means of recovering many patterns that I thought beyond re-drafting. To my photographer Orlando Gualtieri and his long-suffering assistant Miranda Pibworth, thank you for all those times that you held my hand (and fed me as well), and lastly to the lacemakers, of both past generations for their legacy, and to those of the present who have tried out patterns of no little difficulty. On this account may I offer Julia Woods of Plantagenet Lacemakers and Gwenna Jones of Chiltern Lacemakers my sincere gratitude.

I have dedicated my book to my family, and here I should like to include by name those who have especially supported my efforts. My dear husband Ken, who despite ill health has somehow kept the house stable while I hid in a word-processor, my daughter Tessa who withstood demands to proof read at midnight, and my two sons Nick and Jason, who good-naturedly accepted main meals at 9.0 p.m., and washed their own socks with equanimity. This one's for you kids!

1 ARRIVALS

When we arrived in Milton Keynes, we had no idea of what was in store for us. My husband was in the Army and we had been in Germany for a year when sudden changes in our lives brought us to Buckinghamshire. We had never even visited this area before, and it seemed all concrete cows and roundabouts, before I realized that chance had landed us in the centre of an area unparalleled in England's lacemaking history.

The New Town of Milton Keynes, named after a small local village, seems to hang like a kite when viewed on a map, suspended from its corners

Map, produced to accompany a Pigot's directory (1841) showing the proximity of the Lace Villages of three counties

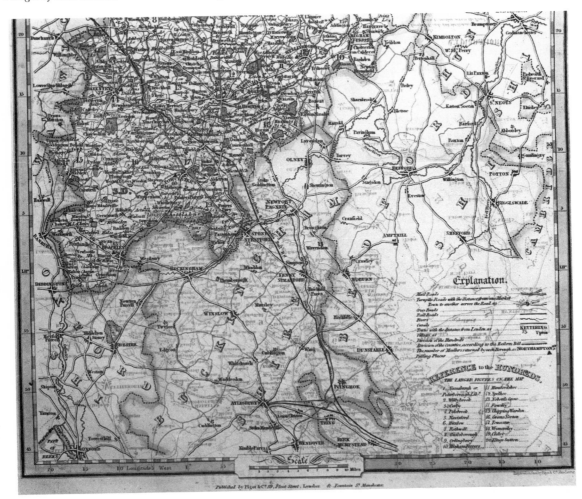

by the established towns of Stony Stratford, Newport Pagnell, and Bletchley. From the Roman occupation onwards, a succession of transport developments has left this part of England more than adequately supplied with road, river, rail and canal links to the outside world; a fact that has influenced both the history of the area and the traditional occupations of the inhabitants.

A Roman road, Watling Street, which originates in Wroxester on the Welsh borders, runs down the western flank of the New Town, providing a swift route to London and beyond and making this area almost medieval commuter territory. The River Ouse meanders its way from Bedfordshire along the county border of Northamptonshire and Buckinghamshire, and the Grand Union Canal ascends steadily from London, through the Blisworth Tunnel and on to Coventry and Birmingham, providing a route for the products of the Industrial Revolution, including machine lace! By the time the railways came north, the entire area had developed its own travel industry, providing inns and hostelries, goods and services for those passing through the region.

When the M1 motorway was driven through the countryside it served to divert traffic away from the villages, returning them from chaos to some semblance of normality; and the development of by-passes and ring roads has returned our 'Laceland' – as the area was christened by Thomas Wright – to a state in which one can visit, explore and at points recapture the feel of the Lace Villages of the eighteenth century.

Deep controversy still surrounds the introduction of lacemaking to this country, and many fictions have grown from Victorian attempts to rationalize the event. Perhaps we should accept that we may never know the truth, but it is important to look at the early foundations of the industry, so that we may understand on what traditions the nineteenth-century revival was based.

It is a matter of record that during the fifteenth and sixteenth centuries refugees escaping from religious persecution began to arrive in Britain by the hundreds. They first came in 1563 from the Low Countries, many escaping the Inquisition visited upon them by Phillip II of Spain. It was noticeably the merchant class who attracted his attention, not only for their religion, but also for the large amounts of money and goods that fell to the state as their owners perished. Many, therefore, fled to the friendlier shores of Britain taking all they could carry and often bringing with them their workers, who, if left behind, would undoubtedly have suffered in the wake of their employers' departure.

Amongst these merchants and dealers in fine textiles, were lace dealers and their lacemakers, and it cannot be coincidence that where they settled our own lacemaking industries sprang up, despite many arguments claiming a lace industry wholly indigenous to Britain.

A succession of religious divisions on the Continent eventually brought in the French Huguenots, who had suffered terrible persecution after the Revocation of the Edict of Nantes in 1685. Their pillow lace industry was

established in the Midlands, despite the huge amounts of needlepoint and pillow lace still being imported from the Continent.

'English' lace, at that time, consisted of versions of drawn threadwork; certainly whitework and cutwork of a very high standard had been produced here for many years and (although needlepoint lace was never developed commercially) Hollie Point, our own needle lace, flourished. Of course, a working knowledge of needlelace techniques was clearly understood by many embroiderers, one of whom may have been Katherine of Aragon, herself a resident of Ampthill, Bedfordshire, while she awaited her divorce from Henry VIII.

In Victorian times a popular story held that Kat stitch, the ground most favoured for black Bucks Point was named after Queen Katherine; some Victorians even put forward the argument that she herself instructed the villagers in how to make bobbin lace, but that seems unlikely. However dishonoured and disgraced, Katherine had been Queen, and although she was an acknowledged embroideress of great skill, it is unlikely that, even had she possessed a working knowledge of bobbin lacemaking, she would have taught the common populace.

The resettlement of refugees from other lacemaking countries confused the facts even more, with several different types of lace being made in the same geographical location. However, it seems fair to comment that where the refugee lacemakers settled, our own 'indigenous' lacemaking areas became established.

OPPOSITE: Cottages typical of the region

Bone bobbins of circa 1841

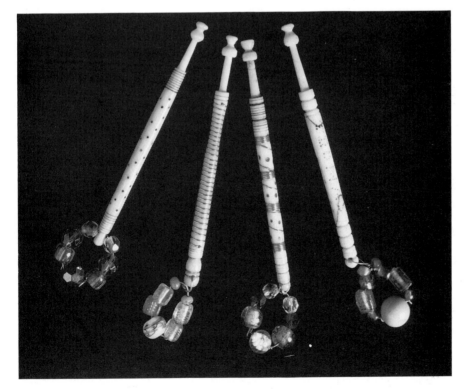

Victorian bobbin winder (photograph courtesy of the Cowper and Newton Museum)

Hundreds of years later, styles of lace now accepted as 'British' can clearly be seen to possess techniques in common with those 'imported' with the refugee populace. However, over many years, lacemakers adapted patterns and techniques in such a way that the lace developed characteristics unique to the area in which it was being made. Despite this, clear comparisons can be made between, for example, Bucks Point and the Lille ground used during the seventeenth century. Point d'Esprit (or spotted ground) is a Point Ground with 'tallies'; similarly, resemblances can be found between fine Brussels lace and the Honiton tradition, although Downton lace is possibly nearer to the original 'import' than the wider developments of Buckinghamshire lace. This is because the Downton lacemakers, true to tradition, protected their patterns, did not hand them on or adapt them and, even today, still work the lace in the Continental fashion, with the footside of the lace on the left.

As Bucks Point was my prime interest in lacemaking, I was greatly intrigued by the area, and my non-stop questions must have greatly amused the local people. For years I had nursed the ambition to do more with my lace, to improve my understanding of the craft, and to visit traditional lacemaking areas. Suddenly all this and more was possible, so, rounding up all the books I could find and arming myself with old maps, I began to research the subject, and in no time I had taken myself and my questions out to the villages.

2 CHANGES

As an occupation, lacemaking was subject not only to the whims and fancies of those who could afford to buy the lace. Surges in demand overturned whole industries, the main causes being changes in fashion, taxation, religion and politics. Laws were passed regarding the use of lace; for instance, one could not be buried in it. One enterprising lacemaker applied for permission to make a fine wool lace specifically for the adornment of the dead and a new industry grew up as a result. To protect the livelihood of our own lacemakers Continental imports were confiscated in the street. Cromwell banned the wearing of any lace, and green lace seen on a pair of shoes was blamed for 'arousing passions'. The expense caused argument between husband and wife (see Pepys' diary, or a modern household after a laceday), and bodies were turned out of coffins in order to smuggle it into the country. Patterns were protected jealously, for the lifestyle of whole communities revolved around the teaching of the craft, the drafting of designs, and the making and marketing of the village products.

By the seventeenth century fashionable Court dandies were sporting the lace of the Midlands, as well as fine Mechlin, and because the lace industry was within reasonable travelling distance of London, men and ladies of fashion started to order lace for their specific requirements. Designers were in demand, and fashions in lace were under their control, with the additional influence of the refugee lacemakers coming to the fore with each new influx. The dealers of London must have been pleased to cut out the uncertainty associated with importing lace across the Channel, even if it meant that they had to journey around the inns attending sales themselves.

Eighteenth-century Mechlin (author's collection)

In spite of periods of recession, by the end of the eighteenth century the sole industry of hundreds of villages in this area was making lace, and perhaps it was this concentration of effort that caused such tremendous hardship as the rise of the Lace Machine took place. From the end of the eighteenth century the Industrial Revolution gained momentum, and by 1812 John Heathcoat, a frame knitter, had established an industry – despite the Luddites wrecking his machinery and almost killing him – producing a net which well served the purposes of the Honiton lacemakers, allowing them to discard the laborious practice of joining their hand-made sprigs together with Trolly Net.

By 1841 successive developments had seen both the 'pusher' machine, which truly imitated pillow lace for the first time, and (using principles ascribed to Jacquard) the Leavers Machine. These technological advances owed some thanks to the pillow lacemaker, whose product was ruthlessly unpicked to examine its construction. The great Victorian engineers thus added another triumph to machine production and, to add insult to injury, their product was transported to London right through traditional lacemaking country.

Machine lace was faster, wider, and so much cheaper than traditional lace that lacemakers began to suffer enormous hardship. Traditional lacemakers in the Midlands make strip lace and the width of the work produced is governed by the width of the lace pillow. To make a dress length in Bucks Point or in Bedfordshire lace would mean attempting to work across a width sufficient to produce the material required. This would be so impractical as to defy description. A lacemaker working on sectional lace such as Honiton or Brussels could have pieced together a large width suitable for dressmaking, but would still have had to put the work out to many women in order to gather the number of 'sprigs' needed. Then would come the labour intensive necessity of 'joining' to make the whole, which would have taken months of work, employed upwards of 20 people and cost an enormous sum of money, thus restricting the potential customers to just a few extremely wealthy women. But even in 1860 a machine could make a dress width in minutes. There was no joining, and the cost was as low as 6d per yard. Thus, when the machines of the mid nineteenth century started to turn out wider widths of lace than had ever been available within the pocket of the average lace wearer, the machine lace gained great popularity.

In 1830, on the visit of Queen Adelaide (wife of William IV) to Stowe (the home of the Duke of Buckingham) local lacemakers petitioned her to wear more English bobbin lace and support their industry. The Queen agreed and for a while it seemed to help, but by the time Queen Victoria and Prince Albert visited in 1845 the industry was struggling again, and even their support was of little use against a world that was being speeded up, mechanized, and generally moving far away from the elegance of dress that incorporated bobbin lace.

Lace thread at this time was imported through the Wash (the North

Black parasol cover

Sea inlet on the east coast) and brought into Bedford by boat. Linen thread is spun from flax and there is little doubt that whole strains of the plant may have been lost to disease and to more intensive methods of farming. Demand has always been for more lace for less money and at greater speed, and where the plants that produced the finest thread were also the most prone to disease, the economy of the times would have dictated a change to another more vigorous strain of flax, despite any subsequent loss of quality. It is also possible that whole strains of flax were deliberately discarded in favour of a faster cropping, but coarser-fibred, plant. Despite growth in technology, handspinning produced a quality of thread that has never been bettered, but production of fine white linen thread depended first on the quality of the fibre and then on sitting in a damp cellar, spinning in comparative darkness to preserve the texture and the pure white colour.

As a result of these changes lace patterns were enlarged to accommodate new coarser materials; even the advent of cotton failed to reverse this trend. Recent years have seen deniers of cotton discontinued for economic reasons and so patterns will have to be adapted once more. Of course it goes without saying that then as now there were differing standards of lacemaking, and thicker threads were widely used throughout the industry for 'utility lace', but whereas in those days linen was available in fine gauges as well, today we must make do with cottons or silks.

Despite this, there were designers who managed to excel, and quite a flutter of interest was stirred when the Bedford workers started to make the designs attributed to Thomas Lester. The lace that Lester produced is unparalleled in its beauty. Not only were Lester's designs outstanding, with floral work and ornate grounds incorporated into the Bedford tradition (without losing the essential techniques of Bedfordshire lace itself) but he also managed to appeal to the Victorian sense of novelty, by including in his designs ostriches, eagles and other more exotic creatures!

The deliberate introduction of faster working patterns was made in the nineteenth century when Bedford lacemakers were encouraged to adopt plaiting techniques introduced from Malta. Many of the older workers were upset by the changes and preferred to cling on to the 'Old Point'. Torchon patterns started to emerge at this time, again as an exercise in faster production, but here Bucks Point remained the favourite, despite increasing difficulties in getting the fine thread necessary for its manufacture.

The decline of lacemaking as a way of life was dictated primarily by the adoption of a more utilitarian style of dress, and as a result lacemaking has now made the transition from industrial process to leisure pursuit. One aspect of this change has given us the time to study lace, to make design innovations, and to improve the quality of the actual manufacture. Improved communications give us access to different disciplines, and allow us to integrate ideas and techniques from other areas into our patterns . . . something that would never have happened in the last century!

3 EMBERTON AND THE INDUSTRIAL SCHOOL

Well within the sight of Olney Church, just across the water meadows on the road to Chicheley, lies the village of Emberton. Emberton is a small place, so close to Olney as to prevent any further growth, and sited so that the popular Emberton Park (watersports and caravan centre) is easily accessible to those entering Olney. It occurred to me that it would be an ideal place to base oneself for a touring holiday of the Lace Villages, right on the outskirts of Olney, within easy walking distance of the town and the Cowper and Newton Museum. Within a ten mile (16 km) radius of Emberton one could visit Weston Underwood, Sherington, Emberton, Newport Pagnell, Stoke Goldington, and would only have to stretch a little further to include Hanslope, Stony Stratford, and the Northampton villages.

Emberton village, Buckinghamshire

That in itself should demonstrate how concentrated were the lacemaking regions. What is a convenient distance today, was a journey of

a day or more in the eighteenth century, and the inability to travel or communicate with ease restricted the growth of the lace districts to those areas where lace could be economically collected. It is not surprising, therefore, to find dealers preferring to support lacemakers in villages close to home, Emberton's lace finding its way to Olney almost by default.

The School of Industry at Emberton owed its existence to common difficulties facing parish councils nationwide, who were responsible for administering the Poor Law Act, under which landowners, employers and the inhabitants of each village made contributions to the rate, out of which each parish looked after its own poor. A sudden rise in the number of families dependent on Parish Relief caused grave concern to many parish councils, who were financially unable to cope, and despite laws being passed in 1819 and 1820 there was little improvement; certainly none of it helped genuine claimants to better their situation.

Amongst those who believed in self-help was the Reverend Thomas Fry of Emberton. Determined to assist those in genuine need by offering training and the hope of obtaining a position in service, he sought sponsors to build homes on charity land, and then launched into the refurbishment of the Village Institute. It was a remarkable accomplishment; labour was provided by the village paupers, and tools, implements, materials and skills by sponsors supporting his aims. Eventually, the Institute housed four schools: an Evening School, Sunday School, a Saturday Working School and a Day School, to which six carefully chosen children of dependants on the Poor Relief were sent. Those who refused to send their children to the school had their money stopped! You might think that the Emberton Industrial School took a hard line with parents, who had virtually to sign away their rights to their children in order to remain on the Poor Relief, but they must have realized how much better their situation would be with a child trained and comfortably established in service.

The funds raised from sponsors and a small levy on the parishioners provided many necessities such as clothing and tutoring. The sponsors formed a Board of Governors and, despite losing one teacher to drink, most of the children received a good training for life. However, few of the sponsors actually took school apprentices as servants and they had to compete in a more open labour market than that originally envisaged by the Reverend Fry. The school continued from 1821 to 1832, when it closed down hard on the heels of a cholera outbreak, although it is not clear whether that event played any part in its demise. At that time the Poor Law changed yet again, and the moment may have seemed opportune to abandon this experiment.

One of the minutes of a meeting held in January 1822 stated that the 'children shall be employed in the manufacture of lace, be taught needlework, plain cooking, washing, ironing . . .'. Its inclusion in the curriculum shows that lacemaking was considered a fit employment for children under the age of 12, the older ones being expected to concentrate on domestic training. In the event, it became clear that in lacemaking areas considerable persuasion was needed to part the lacemaker from her pillow and in most cases the lace pillow won in the end; by the 1841 census, many of the former pupils of the school had turned their backs on life in service and had returned to their homes to take up lacemaking. Certainly, by the end of the nineteenth century many of the women worked for the Bucks Cottage Workers' Agency (BCWA), and Harry Armstrong (the owner of the BCWA) and Thomas Wright (a local lace writer and historian) were well-known visitors to the village.

Lace is still made in the area, and in the nearby village of Sherington there is a very well-attended lace group, with the decided benefits of having a supplier in the village who is one of their founding members. I recently spent a lovely evening with this group; further details are given in Chapter 14.

Several years ago, a friend attending an auction in Sherington telephoned me and asked if I wanted to share in a bid for some lace bobbins. Unable to get there myself I agreed and collected about 20 bone bobbins for a very reasonable sum. None of them were very rare but all were in good condition, the two named ones that I particularly liked being 'Isaac Wright' and 'George Jordan'. Unfortunately, no-one seems to know the history of

Sherington cottages

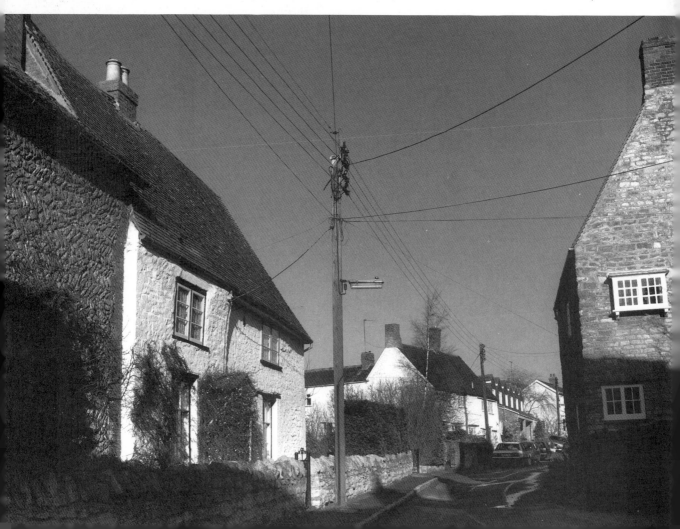

the bobbins, and I have been unable to trace Sherington's lace industry but the two men worked for both the Bucks Cottage Workers' Agency run in Olney and the North Bucks Lace Association in Newport Pagnell. This fact I gathered when I was visiting Renny Lodge, a geriatric hospital, where I heard a very elderly lady say that her mother started making lace at five years old in North Crawley, from where these lacemakers came; and later moved to Sherington where she had to change industries, and didn't much like the patterns or the organizer!

*North Crawley
lacemakers*

OPPOSITE: *Emberton lappett worked by Alwena Jones*

Lappett pricking – taken from an original parchment in the author's collection – originating in Emberton

4 THE TRUTH
ABOUT OLNEY

'Yon cottager who weaves at her own door,
Pillow and bobbins all her little store;
Content, though mean, and cheerful if not gay;
Shuffling her threads about the live-long day;
Just earns a scanty pittance, and at night
Lies down secure, her heart and pocket light.'

Extract from *Truth* (lines 317–336) by William Cowper

One place name synonymous with the lace trade is that of Olney. Olney is a beautiful town, built mainly of stone, with buildings of many different periods nestling together as if by design. There is ample parking, wide pavements, a large market square, and many antique shops hidden away up narrow alleyways. Here you may find lace and lacemaking artefacts, for Olney has been associated with the lace industry from the time the Huguenots arrived.

In 1764 a new curate was appointed to the village. He was an eccentric character, whose previous employments had taken him from being Captain of a slave trader ship to being tide surveyor in Liverpool, where, following a

Olney High Street, from the market end

Traditional cap

minor stroke, he entered the ministry. This was John Newton, who was so charismatic a preacher that his parishioners flocked in their hundreds to hear him tell the stories of his adventuring days and previous wickedness; eventually making it necessary for a special gallery to be erected in the Church to accommodate the numbers. During his 15-year ministry in Olney, he was often to be seen in his old sailor's coat making the rounds of his parishioners, many of whom were penniless, uneducated lacemakers. In the company of William Cowper, who was to become known as the 'lacemaker's poet', he held weekly prayer meetings at a private house near the church, and it was during these that Cowper was made aware of the dreadful social circumstances in which the lacemakers lived.

He became involved in the dreadful struggle against poverty, although he realized that whole families were dependent on the lace trade, and that to try and persuade the women of the town into other work was almost impossible. At one point he commented on this to John Newton, who was trying to find a children's nurse, saying that 'the only thing a girl would dandle on her knee in these parts, was a lace pillow'. The lacemakers of Olney were in such desperate straits in 1780 that Cowper wrote of their plight: 'I am an eyewitness of their poverty and do know that hundreds of this little town are upon the point of starving and that the most unremitting industry is but barely sufficient to keep them from it. There are nearly one thousand and two hundred lacemakers in this beggarly town'.

Whilst all this was going on, other methods of lacemaking were being devised and by 1810, with the pusher machine making a recognizable lace, designers were having to think up ways of attracting more custom. It was quite obvious that smaller items were easier to sell, and John Millward, a lace designer of Olney, turned his talents to looking for a small, speedily made and yet extremely desirable and functional product, and came up with the idea of lace crowns for muslin caps. Millward caps became a byword in the lacemaking history of Olney; the manufacture of the cap crowns from about 1820 did much to help the craft survive a bad period of recession and ensured that the best design in Bucks Point was used and that standards were not allowed to fall. Millward took his designs to the Great Exhibition in 1851 where he won a richly deserved gold award, exports of the cap crowns to the Americas continuing until the Civil War in 1860. Another Olney designer during this period was William Soul, who was a close friend of John Millward, and together these two men earned great recognition for the beauty of their designs.

In the wake of the Industrial Revolution many women were beginning to enter new professions, and the numbers of skilled lacemakers dropped. However, the craftswomen who remained at home continued to seek ways to popularize what was now a truly cottage industry.

Late in the nineteenth century, lacemakers at their cottage doors, working in the sun, attracted another type of interest from those seeking to capture the last images of a dying trade, and it is an undoubted fact that the new art of photography induced many of the local lacemakers to pose,

Bucks lacemakers

Martha Hines at Ravenstone

probably in the hope that the photographs would encourage visitors to purchase their lace. I have come across several postcards featuring lacemakers working at their pillows, and examination reveals the same lacemakers posed in different locations.

There is in existence a photograph of 20 Bucks lacemakers whose combined ages are 1,600 years, each one being conveniently named and her age given; this was published by the BCWA in a booklet entitled *A Sixteenth Century Industry* and when a copy fell into my hands I discovered, to my amusement, several of the same ladies posed either by different photographers or in different settings. One such postcard has a hand-tinted sky, and features Martha Hines aged 74 in the village of Ravenstone. She is shown seated, making lace at the cottage door, hard on the edge of a badly made up road that no self respecting lacemaker would have taken her pillow within a mile of!

Ravenstone lies on the direct route from Stoke Goldington to Olney, the route that Harry Armstrong took when he moved his Bucks Cottage Workers' Agency to Olney in 1909. The Agency needed improved postal services and bought a larger building in the High Street, which became known as the Lace Factory. Lace, however, was never made here although lace 'joiners' may have pieced together the lengths that were sorted, measured, rolled and packed, to be sent out on approval.

The Bucks Cottage Workers' Agency's handbook used sketches and photographs of the types of lace made to invite orders and was nothing short of an Edwardian clothing catalogue. Priced in both pounds sterling and dollars (showing that the agency not only expected to trade with the Americans, but positively invited the chance) it is full of designs and ideas for the use of lace. It includes many exhortations to the prospective purchaser, from frequent requests not to cut out the drawings in the catalogue, to an interesting suggestion under a drawing of an elaborate high-necked blouse made entirely from insertions of lace joined together: 'Made in all sizes. This lace could be unpicked and used for other purposes if desired at any time. Pillow lace wears for many years.' This, to my certain knowledge, was quite a common practice, lace being so expensive that when a dress wore out or became unfashionable the lace trim was removed and the lace re-attached to another garment. I have a large collection of mid-Victorian and Edwardian lace, amongst which I found seventeenth-century Point d'Angleterre and eighteenth-century Mechlin displaying the signs of removal from one garment, presumably to be saved for another purpose.

The Cowper and Newton collection displayed in Gilpin House (the home of William Cowper's manservant and part of the Cowper and Newton Museum) contains lace made throughout the duration of the Bucks Cottage Workers' Agency. It also houses many of the artefacts of the BCWA, one of which is a splendid 'flash-stool' with rush hutches for spare lights, presented

The Lace Factory at Olney, home of the Bucks Lace industry and the BCWA, founded by Harry Armstrong and most definitely not in existence in the sixteenth century (see detail below)!

to the museum by Harry Armstrong on 17 September 1917. Whole lengths of lace as sent out by the agency are kept here, and I was allowed access to many of the town's treasures, so that I could demonstrate the intricate designs common to those times.

A satin baby jacket (courtesy of the Cowper and Newton Museum)

OVERLEAF
TOP: *A collection of samples lent to the Cowper and Newton Museum by Elizabeth Wright*

BELOW: *Beautiful Bucks Point*

Set of cuffs from the Cowper and Newton reserve collection

LEFT: *A flash stool presented to the Cowper and Newton Museum by Harry Armstrong in 1917*

RIGHT: *A model flash light*

BELOW: *Bedfordshire Lace (ordered by the yard!)*

A Lille cap from the Cowper and Newton collection

The Cowper and Newton Museum* was brought into being by Thomas Wright, author of *Romance of the Lace Pillow*, *Romance of the Shoemaker* and *Romance around Stony Stratford*. He ran the Cowper School at the rear of Orchard Side, and pestered the owner of Cowper's home, Mr Colinridge, to give the house to the townsfolk for a museum. Eventually, Mr Colinridge gave in, a town meeting was called, and the gift of the property accepted. However, quite a scene ensued when, after the voting in of the first board of Trustees, Thomas Wright's name was noticeably absent from the list! He protested so emphatically that eventually he was appointed Secretary of the Trust, his family following him on the Board of Trustees for several generations.

A more tangible line with the lacemaking past of Olney lies in the fact that a former curator of the museum, Sylvia Bull, is herself a lacemaker and was a member of the Olney Lace Circle. A very active lace group, they hold regular lacedays and encourage young lacemakers to take up the craft. Meetings are held weekly in the museum itself and amongst their members they have a supplier, Iris Martin, who has recently moved from her high street shop to Farthing Cottage in the intriguingly named 'Clickers Yard'.

*For more details regarding the Cowper and Newton Museum please refer to p. 134.

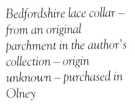

*Bedfordshire lace collar –
from an original
parchment in the author's
collection – origin
unknown – purchased in
Olney*

'Orchardside', the home of William Cowper and now the Cowper and Newton Museum

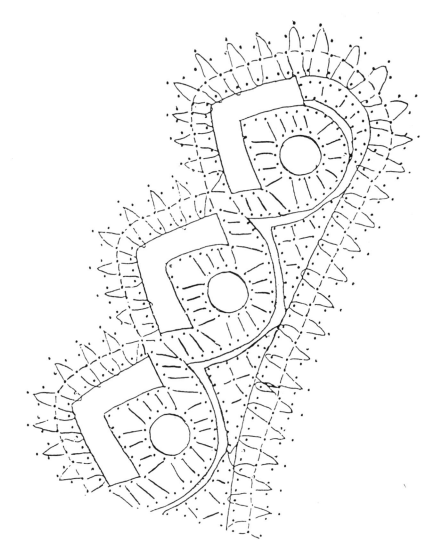

LEFT AND OPPOSITE:
A traditional Bedford collar from Olney, taken from an original pricking in the author's collection

5 NEWPORT PAGNELL

On leaving Olney take the road to Weston Underwood and, as you climb the hill, be sure and look back at Olney Church lying in the valley below. You can see right through the piercings on the steeple, a sight said to have inspired the creation of 'Church Window' bobbins.

Weston Underwood is typical of lacemaking villages at the end of the nineteenth century. The warm-coloured stone cottages, the quiet streets and the companiable peace of the village has been little disturbed by the twentieth century. In at least one cottage there are still lacemakers, and as you pass Bolbec House and go through the pineapple-topped gates into the High Street it should come as no surprise to see the plaque on the village green which declares Weston Underwood to be the 'Best Kept Village in Britain'.

Sitting squarely between Stoke Goldington and Olney, this village is where William Cowper came after John Newton left Olney. Still surrounded by his beloved lacemakers, he penned some of his most famous works here from Cowper's Alcove (a gazebo in a field behind the High Street, erected in 1753 by the Throckmorton family) and the poet's influence can be seen in Cowper's Lodge, and 'Cowper's Oak' (the village pub).

Throughout the village, high walls surround private gardens, and one long stretch of wall facing Bolbec House caused me to remember the Lace Tell:

> A boy down at Olney looked over a wall,
> Saw nineteen little golden girls playing at ball

Of course in this instance the 'little golden girls' were the lace pins to be set in the lace, but I often wonder about that wall; did Cowper hear such naïve rhymes being chanted by the village children as they returned from lace school?

It is no more than four miles (6 km) from Weston Underwood to Newport Pagnell, where the eighteenth-century industry grew to such proportions that, in addition to the London merchants, the village had its own lace buyers. Listed in a eighteenth-century diary are their names: Banson (whose wife was treated for lunacy), Botty and Cosins.

The Revd William Coles' diary (1765–7) mentions lace buyers James and Nathaniel Cartwright in connection with Newport Pagnell. Both resident in Bletchley, one brother would travel, buying and selling lace, whilst the other 'stayed in the country and looked after the lacemakers', calling at the cottages weekly to measure the work and strike off the lace. The lacemaker would be given the pattern, threads and other equipment for the manufacture of 'yardage'; on strike-off day the lace would be marked with sealing wax, two strips being marked on the lace and the lace cut between. The colour of the sealing wax would denote the village from whence the lace had come, and a number would be affixed to the lace to identify the lacemaker. The lace being cut off at the back of the pillow would not disturb the lacemaker, who could simply continue working her length, but this proved to be a wasteful method of collection that had to be improved in the nineteenth century. Another reason for this marking of the lace meant that the lacemaker could not make any profit on the side, for she had to ensure that the waxed end of the lace was visible on the next collection.

A selection of prickings on parchment, mainly from the nineteenth century

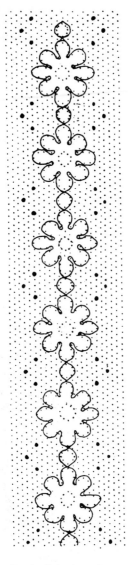

The work was boring, repetitive, badly paid and exhausting, and the pale faces of the lacemakers of Newport were commented on in the eighteenth century. Thomas Pennant wrote in *The Journey from Chester to London* (1779):

> It [Newport Pagnell] *flourishes greatly, by means of the lace manufacture, which we stole from the Flemings, and introduced with great success into this county. There is scarcely a door to be seen, during Summer, in most of the towns, but what is occupied by some industrious pale-faced lass; their sedentary trade forbidding the rose to bloom in their sickly cheeks.*

The indentures of Eleanor Gibbs (1711) state that she was to be taught 'the *mistery* of making lace'. I persistently mis-read this as 'the *misery* of making lace' (and maybe I am right!) but still agricultural wages could not compete, for a good lacemaker could make between 1s and 1s 3d a day which was sufficient inducement for many.

On 11 June 1767 William Cole wrote: 'Drank coffee with Mr Cartwright, who had strained his Ankle in coming yesterday from Newport Lace Fair, where I suppose he got drunk, as his Finger was hurt & his Great Coat all over Dirt & his other clothes also. Now & then he will get fuddled.' The injury to the ankle must have been quite severe, for a month later, on 25 July 1767, the diary makes note that on a 'Very rainy Day. Mr N Cartwright set off for his long Journey into the North & by Glocester, with above £1,000 of lace, tho' very lame with his Ankle.'

Lace was still in the forefront of masculine fashion, and mentioned in Cole's Diary are various purchases of lace: 'An hat for Tom with silver lace' and 'lent Tom 2 guineas to buy lace of[f] Tom Cosins'.

In 1830 the Lace Merchants of Newport Pagnell are listed as:

Ayers John D.	St John Street
Clarkson Thomas	Green
Cripps William	St John Street
Hanscombe William	High Street
Keep William	High Street
Ladds Christr. (pearl lace)	High Street
Marshall James	Tickford End.

I think it likely that the reference to pearl lace should read 'purl' lace, to denote that Christopher Ladds' lacemakers made Bucks Point, the 'purls' or picots along the headside being greatly in demand.

In 1870 William Cowley purchased from the fellmonger, Thomas Book, a site backing on to the river, where he established his parchment business. Parchment would have been a common writing material at the establishment of the lace industry, lacemakers pricking their patterns on to off-cuts. Its properties have ensured the survival of many old designs

Bucks Point insertion from the North Bucks Lace Association

although there is little possibility of dating such patterns from the look or feel of any one piece. A pattern issued by the Bucks Lace Association in 1897 could have been pricked yesterday (it came as no surprise to me to discover that the Domesday Book also has pages which look almost new instead of the 900 years old they really are). Parchment today is used for calligraphy, the making of all types of drums and binding books, although I did obtain some for pricking. My comments on this, and the tips I was given at Cowleys on the care of old prickings are to be found in Chapter 15.

In 1897 the Buckingham Lace Industry was so successful that Miss M. Burrowes was asked by Mrs W. Carlysle, the wife of the local MP, to help the workers around Newport Pagnell, who by this time had experienced the damage done to the bobbin-lace trade by the machine lace industry. Lack of organization, no lace designer and few dealers left the workers at Newport with little in the way of orders, and decreasing outlets for their work.

Miss Burrowes agreed to act as the temporary Secretary to the North Bucks Lace Association (established to represent the interests of the Midlands Lace Association). She patiently corrected patterns, instructed

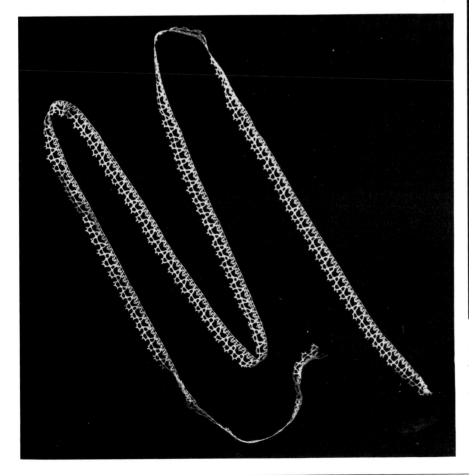

ABOVE: *The lace from the pricking opposite, worked in two slightly different ways*

LEFT: *Ninepin edging, for children to work by the yard*

lacemakers about selecting quality threads and issued her own designs, with the result that enough orders were secured to allow her to hand over the reigns to a Miss Hewley in 1902. Despite this, the general trade continued to decline steadily and when the First World War (1914–18) broke out lace pillows were discarded and the organized lace industry died, along with many of the village women in the 1917 influenza epidemic.

Phyllis Martin (aged 72 at the time of writing) lost her mother in the epidemic when she was only five years old, and the eldest of three children. She remembers that they eventually moved to a row of cottages off Silver Street, built on the present-day site of Lovat Hall where, at the age of twelve, she first encountered lacemaking, which by this time was reduced to a few women making lace for private orders.

Her neighbour, Mrs Wright, taught her to make a ninepin edging, which she sold for about 4s. More orders followed but her stepmother's poor health meant that Phyllis was often too busy to make lace. When she left school at 14 her interests were primarily musical; she gave up lace until a few years ago when she joined a class and discovered that she had not forgotten everything.

As for Newport itself, gone are the days when the town had its own rail service, the old line is now a 'Railway walk', and a modern Fire Station has been built on the site of the terminus. The streets that once had the odd car, a daily bus, and pedestrians or pony carts, lie just off the M1 motorway services, and the High Street retains little evidence of the gracious days of long dresses and lace. However, a walk down Silver Street allows you to imagine life as it was and when you reach the junction of Silver Street and Caldecote Street a Tudor timbered cottage serves to remind you that in many of these towns and villages it only takes the time to switch off the ignition key and walk to discover the best of our heritage.

6 THE BUCKS COTTAGE WORKERS' AGENCY

During the period 1872–1880 various Acts of Parliament were beginning to cut heavily into the traditional pool of employment for the lace industry – children. The Elementary Education Act of 1872 and the subsequent Factory and Workshops Act left the Industry with little in the way of 'fresh blood' to call on. Better education and the appalling prospects in traditional lacemaking areas, including that of Honiton in Devon, found lacemakers deserting the pillow for employment found mainly in cities or on the outskirts of large towns. The workforce was made up of middle-aged and elderly women, with rather inflexible attitudes, coupled to the fact that, as little future could be seen for an industry competing with machines and Free Trade, designers had ceased to work.

It was hard to see what could be done to improve matters and in the late 1880s a report for the Home Office by A.S. Cole stated the industry to be in a condition of abject depression. In Devon he found that buyers were refusing to accept Honiton lace as genuine because standards had fallen so low and, three years later, when he reported on the Midland industry, he felt that the only hope for the restoration of quality was for travelling teachers to teach the lacemakers on standardized patterns, and to award prizes for the best efforts. There was no response to his suggestions; perhaps his reports were so gloomy that the Home Office could see no reason in sponsoring the industry, and by the 1890s the industry might have failed completely but for the efforts of the local dealers, and the Philanthropic Movement.

Inspired by some sense of guilt over their enhanced social position, men and women of the leisured class had started to pursue the Philanthropic aims. Poverty, ignorance, disease and hopelessness amongst the lower social classes was to be wiped out, and rural areas were not exempt from their investigations; even the most romantic amongst them being persuaded that it would be socially acceptable to enter into trade provided that the intention was to help others. In 1883 businessmen and social reformers established the Society for Promoting Industrial Villages and soon their gaze was levelled at the lacemaking villages of the country. A number of organizations sprang into life, to help co-ordinate the collection, sales, and standard of the lace produced, and 'to enhance the happiness of its workers'. The Queen gave several of these industries her patronage, and did much to persuade the nobility to take an active interest, and names such as the Hon. Rose Hubbard, Lady Inglefield and The Countess Spencer began to appear on the letterheadings of Lace Associations.

Of course the romantics of the era became involved, and several publications on the subject appeared, one of which, in the magazine *Madame* (15 October 1898), read thus:

> *There are many pretty villages in Bedfordshire and their charm is often enhanced by the quaint pictures the lacemakers present to the passers-by, as, seated outside their cottage doors they ply their favourite industry.*
>
> *Here an old dame of eighty-three has taken her pillow on its three-legged stand to the gate of her ivy-clad house, and works away busily in the sunshine; whilst opposite her, the winder on her knee, the daughter fills the bobbins for her mother's use. There, on the threshold of her tiny house, where she spends her life with a cat as her only companion, is an elderly woman: her husband is dead, the children are out in the world, and yet she is happy; her thoughts, her hopes, her fears seem to work themselves into the lace as it grows beneath her fingers. What a boon for the women who have few interests in the world to be able to work until the last.*

To those of us who know the reality of the hardships suffered during that era, this sort of report defies all comment!

Bucks modesty piece (BCWA) (courtesy of the Cowper and Newton Museum)

One of the major problems lay in establishing a nucleus of skilled workers with access to traditional patterns of high quality. The lacemakers would generally have worked the pattern only of *their* village, however inaccurate it had become. Thankfully, however, the Victorians persevered in the 'trueing' and re-drafting of the old patterns to correct the ravages of time, and in designing 'new patterns' in the lace of the region.

Geoff Spencley's paper, *The Lace Associations: Philanthropic Movements to Preserve the Production of Hand-made Lace in Late Victorian and Edwardian England*, reveals an interesting twist to the story. Many lacemakers were only too thankful that the Associations gave them at least some guarantee of employment, but some of the most elderly found it very hard to work the re-drafted patterns, and several plaintive letters from lacemakers survive to highlight this problem:

> *Please I set a wide lace, I down one down. But I could not see to set up, it is so close. I new I should not be asked to do what you wanted, but you see I am over eighty years old, I can't help it.*

Detail of lace opposite

Harry Armstrong's Bucks Cottage Workers' Agency was originally established in the village of Stoke Goldington, on the B526 road to Northampton, which would place him roughly equidistant between Olney, Newport Pagnell and Northampton. This piece from the BCWA handbook gives the reasons for the establishment of the industry:

The founding of the Agency was the outcome of a dire need felt for an institution that would collect and market the productions of the village women, therefore ensuring for them immediate remuneration for their efforts, to add to their husbands scanty income.

Previously Cottage Lace-makers were never certain of being able to dispose of their lace even when made, and this state of things naturally resulted in the industry being considerably curtailed; many workers being forced to lay aside their pillows.

The Agency is maintained as it was started, in the belief that the production of materials by hand for use in the home and for the clothing of its inmates is a great source of happiness to the worker; and has besides, an educational value hardly to be measured.

The Agency is established on a sound financial basis, and being quite SELF SUPPORTING it relieves the workers from any feeling of injured self-respect, or in any way encroaching upon their independence. This is a point of vital importance to a village industry both from the commercial and the lace-makers standpoint.

No subscriptions are asked for, or received.

The Agency has now patrons in all parts of the civilized world, and with the support of the public, hopes to be able to give regular orders to all the lace makers throughout Buckinghamshire, Bedfordshire, and Northamptonshire.

Bedford at its best
(BCWA)

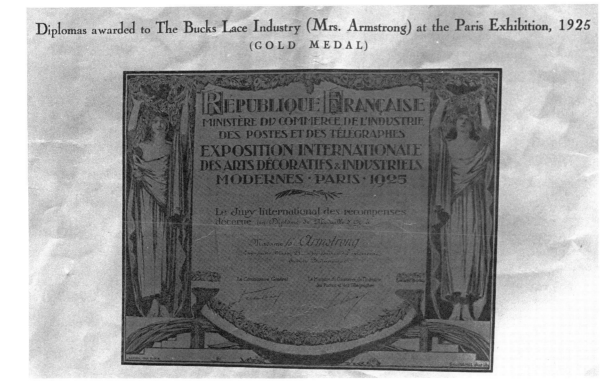

Diplomas awarded to The Bucks Lace Industry (Mrs. Armstrong) at the Paris Exhibition, 1925
(GOLD MEDAL)

A cottage in Stoke Goldington had been rented as an office for the BCWA, and Harry Armstrong and his workers intended to use it to the full. Local buyers were organized and patterns were distributed together with thread and other materials, Harry Armstrong himself undertaking most of this work. He was well aware that the recession in trade had brought about a falling off in standards, for his handbook records that they had been 'closely examining every specimen of lace sent in, pointing out any defects, with suggestions where improvements could be carried out. By following this course determinedly, the lace was gradually brought up to a higher standard of workmanship'.

As standards grew he hit upon the idea of offering a guarantee of workmanship. The lace was distributed made up in six yard (five and a half metres) lengths, folded into half-yard (half-metre) hanks and stitched to a ticket bearing the name of the industry where the lace had been made. This acted as a guarantee and must have impressed the ladies buying the lace, for the postal business boomed and, after one disastrous foray into direct sales, the BCWA concentrated its efforts on the mail order business, advertising through ladies' magazines and journals. Only the very rich could afford lace; many county families sponsored the sale of local lace directly, others indirectly, by postal purchase. Thus, a connection with county families was established and soon Armstrongs were literally forced by pressure of trade to remove their offices to Olney. The improved postal facilities and the ability

BCWA diploma and Gold Award. Other awards won by the Armstrong family were: 1911, Henry Armstrong (The Festival of Empire and Imperial Exhibition, Crystal Palace, London); 1922, Mrs Armstrong (Central Canada Exhibition Association, Ottawa; 1924 and 1925, Mrs Armstrong (British Empire Exhibition, Wembley, London).

to hire clerical staff allowed the BCWA to send their goods all round the world. They exhibited the work of the area to great success, winning the Gold Medal and Diploma at the Festival of Empire and Imperial Exhibition held at the Crystal Palace in 1911.

Names of Huguenot origin still exist in the Stoke Goldington area; Godfrey, from Godfrai, being one definitely bound up with the lacemaking tradition of this village. Descendants of Harry Armstrong still live there, and the village has a strong interest in its history, boasting a society established to research and discuss matters pertinent to Stoke Goldington's past.

Bedford collar pattern from Stoke Goldington

7 TELL A TALE OF CHILDREN HEADS BENT OVER PINS . . .

One of the outstanding sights across the fields of northern Buckinghamshire is the spire of St James the Great at Hanslope. This soaring spire, delicately poised between flying buttresses, is the highest point of the county, visible for miles around, and is a popular climb for more hardy souls on church open days. Having been invited to demonstrate at one of these events, I found myself in the company of many other craft workers, and during the course of the day so many people spoke of family involvement in the industry that I realized that Hanslope was, until comparatively recently, dependent on the money brought in at the lace pillow. In 1838, 800 out of a population of 1,275 brought in a revenue in excess of £8,000, from lacemakers in nearly every family in the village.

St Martin's Church, Hanslope

Bucks Ring Pattern, possibly a suitable edging for a christening robe. This pattern, no. 148, was issued by the North Bucks Lace Association

The industry at Hanslope was big enough to support a number of lace merchants, one of whom, a Mr Phillips, is reputed to have hidden his money in his bedroom floor, making a trapdoor to conceal his guineas. He then, unhappily, proceeded to draw on his hoard until 'all were spent on wine' and died poor, his daughters Nelly and Polly becoming paupers.

There were two lace schools in Hanslope, the first in Long Street where one cottage is still known as Lace Cottage, and the other in Castlethorpe Road. For the children who attended these lace schools life at home was hard, as many as 15 to a cottage, and they had to work, or they starved. Before the Education Act of 1876, children attending lace schools started on the narrowest edgings, and often worked for six or seven hours a day, earning just 6d a day. Those children who were slow to learn had their noses rubbed on their pins, and those who were simply inattentive had their hands rapped raw for 'looking off the pillow'. They were not allowed to talk, and the infrequent breaks allowed them only 'ten minutes to scramble [play], and the other to break straw for the stuffing of pillows'.

Lacemaking was not limited to girls, boys and men made lace too, the men working long hours in agriculture and then making lace or winding the bobbins in the evening. Some men took up the craft as a full-time occupation and were listed as such in the militia lists of the times. In 1803 a Hanslope man, George Hancock, was mentioned and from other villages (covered in previous chapters) we have:

1779	lacemaker	Emberton	Charles Cooper
1803	lacemaker	North Crawley	James Cobb

as well as many others in Olney and Newport Pagnell.

Boys, at around the age of 11, would be allowed to take up more 'manly' occupations, perhaps following their fathers at the plough, or becoming an apprentice shoemaker. For one boy, named to me as William Preece, that day could not come too soon. Given his pillow and bobbins to take home to his mother, the Hanslope story has him 'just passing the village well' when temptation beckoned, and in one moment of unholy joy the tiresome pillow went in!! I imagine the village bounds to have been soundly beaten that year, most of the punishment landing on that unfortunate's rear end! Several versions of this tale exist: the boy chucked his pillow down a well at Elstow; in a duck-pond (anonymous); a third claims that he threw his pillow down a well and ran away to sea, but I like the first version, told to me by several different villagers.

Children would have been difficult to encourage in this craft had not a spirit of competition been engendered amongst them, and it was to this purpose that the telling of 'lace tells' was put. It was essential to get the children's attention firmly on the pillow and to achieve some kind of rhythm in their movements, and it was through monotonous chanting that this was achieved. Turning the making of lace into a race against their fellows must have encouraged the youngsters, and several of their lace tells have survived, and been adapted into nursery rhymes. One, which I call a 'teaching tell', goes like this:

> *Needlepin, needlepin, stitch upon stitch,*
> *Work the old lady out of the ditch,*
> *If she is not out as soon as I*
> *A rap on the knuckles will come by and by,*
> *A Horse to carry my lady about,*
> *Must not look off till twenty are out.*

Taken line by line, we can interpret the tell as follows:

> '*Needlepin*': a tool used to make a 'stitch upon stitch': sewing
> '*Work the old lady out of the ditch*: pull your sewing loop through
> '*If she is not out as soon as I*': If you are not as deft as I am
> No interpretation needed for the next line!
> The '*horse*': the stool for '*my lady*': the pillow
> *Must not look off till 20 are out* (do not look off your pillow till you
>   have set 20 pins)

Others were simple rhymes to pass the time and to get the children's fingers working rhythmically as an aid to speed. The tell would be recited at a steady pace, and as the appropriate number (often 19 or 20) was called a silence, known as a 'glum', would fall over all those participating . . . and then the fingers would positively fly to be the first to set the number of pins 'telled'. As the last was set the first child to complete the set would call out, for the added inducement to speed was that they could call the next tell.

Some of the Buckinghamshire Tells were seen as very gruesome, although they would scarcely raise a goose-pimple now, and at least one purports to be the story of a prospective murder, circumvented by the teller of the tale.

It is easy to see how this practice, learnt as a child, was used by adults as an aid to concentration. Any repetitive job benefits from establishing a rhythm, and when your livelihood hung on the speed at which you worked, anything that lifted the spirit, and gave fresh impetus to tiring fingers and eyes would have been used.

Northamptonshire, as a lacemaking county, is not as well known as it ought to be. Casual research into the border villages of Northampton (which can be seen from the spire of St James) revealed lacemakers in their hundreds using patterns in the familiar techniques of both Bedford and Bucks, but the county has not been recognized in the same way as Devon, Buckinghamshire and Bedfordshire. Yet there was a major lace industry here, which won the patronage of Queen Victoria, and whose President was none other than the Countess Spencer.

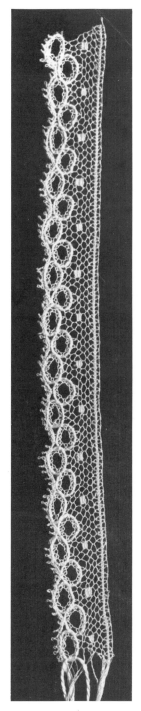

Lace made in Mr Piper's Poly-Cotton 80, to pattern no. 148 (BLA)

8 THE MIDLAND LACE ASSOCIATION

Few people are aware of Northamptonshire as a traditional lacemaking county, in fact, outside of Northampton people themselves, scant recognition is paid to any of the Lace Villages other than those on the periphery of the Bucks/Beds industries.

Where awareness of the Northampton connection does exist it is applied condescendingly to those villages close to the county borders, which are called 'semi-traditional lacemaking villages', whilst the rest of the county is ignored. However, the militia lists of 1777 not only disprove the accuracy of that attitude but make specific references to the 'nine to ten thousand young women and boys employed in lacemaking in Wellingborough and the neighbourhood' (chronicled by James Donaldson in 1794).

Information about traditional occupations can be gathered from such records, and in this case militia lists refer to men between the ages of 18 and 45 (naming the man, his village and his occupation) if fit for military service. Finding lace buyers and lacemen on these lists, I pursued lacemaking history over the county border.

I eventually extracted from the list of 1777 some 28 male lacemakers, eleven from Bozeat, seven from Grendon, three at Ashton, two at Stoke Bruerne, two at Raunds and two at Towcester, leaving one in Kettering. Listed as separate occupations were lace buyers, lacemen and lace dealers, 12 of whom were listed by the constables as being itinerant: four lacemen and one lace buyer at Wellingborough; two lace dealers and one laceman at Northampton; one lace dealer at both Wollaston and Finedon and one laceman each at Bozeat and Yardley Hasting. In addition to these there would also have been a substantial lacemaking industry to support their activities, and in evidence of this a report of considerable numbers of 'females being employed in the making of bobbin lace' was made in 1794.

The Northampton militia list describes 9,000 lacemakers in the Kettering area. This represents a good two-thirds of the entire Huguenot exodus that brought lace into this country 150 years earlier, and as a consequence Northamptonshire deserves recognition as a traditional lacemaking county. Certainly it was recognized as such during the late nineteenth century and the revival of the lace industries.

In 1891 there was an exhibition of needlework and pillow lace at Northampton. Opened by the Duchess of Teck it was a huge success, with at least 500 exhibits of pillow lace, which aroused sufficient interest (and sales) to prompt the formation of the Midland Lace Association. A working

Grand Union Canal, Stoke Bruerne

party to examine the case for the Northampton industry was set up and an exploratory meeting held at St Giles Vicarage, Northampton. The objects of the Association were to 'improve the local manufacture of lace, to provide workers with greater facilities for the sale of their work and more remunerative prices, and to provide instruction in lacemaking' (*Northampton Herald*, 16 January 1897). Stating aims similar to the BCWA, its committee was to include well-known organizers of other local industries, including Mrs Roberts of Spratton, Mrs Chettle and Mrs Bostock of Northampton, Mrs Forest of Princes Risborough, and Mrs Harrison of Paulerspury, their work to be carried out under the care of a President, the Countess Spencer.

Schools were set up to teach the craft, a list of subscribers was established in order to defray the expenses of the Association until it became self-sufficient and the lacemakers of the county were soon fully employed. Perhaps thanks to the aristocratic patronage the lace of the Midlands found keen buyers everywhere, and in the Chicago Exhibition of 1894 it carried off the major prize.

Huge orders were placed, several of which came from very exalted figures; the Duchess of York ordered 330 yards (356 metres) of the 'finest Buckinghamshire Point' and in 1896 the dizzy pinnacle of success was achieved when the secretary of the industry reported that an order from the Queen had been placed, so large that an entire winter's work was guaranteed for many hands.

Bedford lace made in Northampton

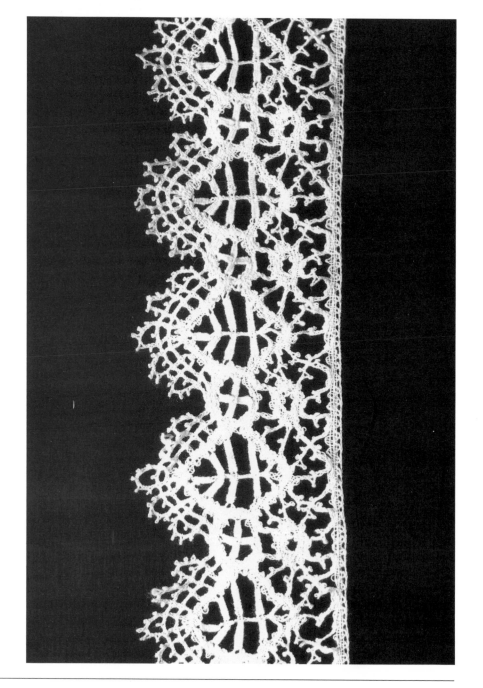

The workers of the Northampton industry were spurred on to further efforts for the Diamond Jubilee, and lace from the county was presented to the Queen, one piece of which, from Blakesley, had a Jubilee inscription worked into it (unfortunately I could find no local record of that inscription). Shortly after this the Midland Association formed another group to take care of their interests in Buckinghamshire; this being the North Bucks Lace Association, and with matters firmly in hand, the lace Association predicted a prosperous future. However, it was not to be long before the meteoric rise was halted.

Mrs Clara Webb, whose mother worked in the Paulerspury industry, well remembered the effect of the unprophesized slump in the industry. By the end of the First World War, changes in fashion had reduced the sales of the Association, with the result that lacemakers were forced once more to sell their work directly. Unfortunately, unless your work was sold through the Associations, you had no guarantee of sale. Clara remembered one hot day walking 15 miles (24 km) to the other side of Towcester with her mother to sell some lace that had been ordered privately. On arriving at her customer's home Mrs Herbert and young Clara were turned away by the servants, the mistress of the house having left word to say that the lace was no longer wanted, fringes being all the rage now!

This must have been a common story and a desperate state of affairs for those who knew no other life, and were too old to adapt, but for others the Lace Age was over, and they did not mourn its passing.

9   PAULERSPURY – PURY END

I could have written an entire book on this interesting pair of villages, if they really are a pair, for it seems that the Pury End now established in its own right may have developed from a cluster of cottages at one end of the larger complex of Paulerspury. Numerous villages in the area have 'ends'; Church End is a frequent description, and means, literally, the houses at the church end of the village, but Pury End is separated from Paulerspury by nearly a half mile (0.8 km), and could have started life as a separate village.

Paulerspury Church

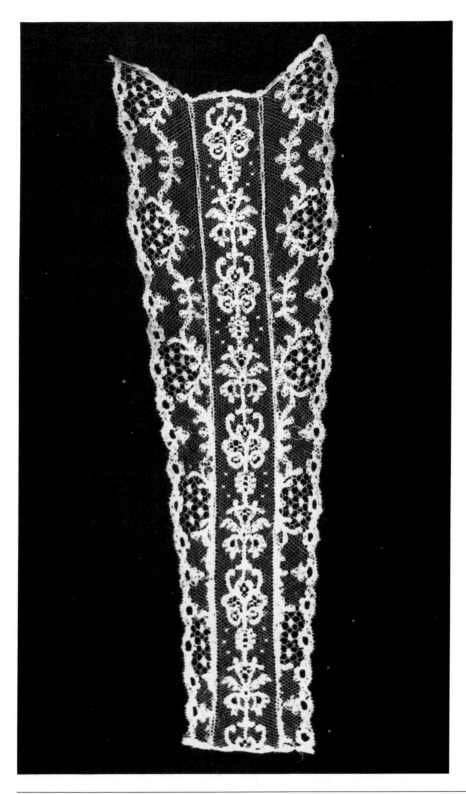

Paulerspury lies on the west side of Watling Street as it runs north to Towcester (Roman Lactodorum), and little can be seen of the village from that road except a few houses and the imposing frontage of Plum Park, a mansion besieged during the Civil War. However, if you take the turning to the village, a few minutes' drive will bring you into contact with the familiar stone dwellings of the region, and into the heart of Paulerspury.

Although quite a small village for a large lace industry, Paulerspury was so efficient that the organizer, Mrs Harrison, was voted on to the committee of the Midland Lace Association in 1897. This village worked both Bucks Point and Bedfordshire lace, selling their work regularly to royalty and to the gentry. Mrs Harrison established a high standard of workmanship by regularly offering prizes for the best pieces of lace produced and many of the village patterns have survived in good order, thanks to the care used in their pricking. Familiar patterns such as the Beehive were worked in the village, and throughout the lifetime of the Midland Lace Association the lacemakers of Paulerspury were kept occupied. However, it is with the satellite village of Pury End that this chapter is mainly concerned, and the lacemakers of Long Row.

Long Row in Pury End

Across the fields from the Paulerspury Church lies the huddle of houses known as Pury End from which many lacemakers worked at the turn of the century, as Paulerspury's industry went into a slow decline.

Mrs Ivy Clarke, born on 24 June 1900 and the seventh of 12 children, recalled the industry clearly, for her mother, Mrs Rogers, was the village pattern-pricker. A skilled lacemaker, Mrs Rogers would prick the patterns of the other villagers for a penny and send the children (with the pattern) scampering back down the street to Long Row, which consisted of 13 cottages joined together, in which lived many of the lacemaking families of this hamlet. Times were hard, and yet Mrs Clarke, the late Mrs Clara Webb, and her niece Mrs Daniels all remembered the companionship and good humour of the inhabitants of Long Row (sometimes referred to as New Row or just the Row).

Mrs Clarke lent me a copy of the *Northampton and County Independent*, dated 21 September 1929, containing a photograph of her mother, Mrs Rogers, her sister, Mrs Smart of Paulerspury, and her mother's sister, Mrs Kingston of Northampton. They are shown busy at the pillow during an exhibition at the Guildhall Road Museum in Towcester. The clipping (unfortunately too dark to reproduce) states: 'one of the objects served by the exhibition was to reveal to many for the first time that Northamptonshire has a great reputation for the making of pillow lace, founded on the skill of many generations of cottage workers, handed down from mother to daughter.' Thomas Pennant, in his *Journey from Chester to London* (1780) wrote:

> The town (Toucester) [sic] is supported by the great concourse of passengers and by a manufacture of lace, and a small one of silk stockings. The first was imported from Flanders, and is carried on with much success in this place, and with skill in the neighboring [sic] country of Buckingham.

Mrs Rogers, who learnt her first stitches at five years of age, was sent to a lace school at the age of seven, where she paid 2d a week for instruction, her mother walking the 12 miles from Paulerspury to Northampton and back to sell the family's work.

In this article, Mrs Rogers said that she attributed the decline of the lace industry to the lack of patience and perseverance in the young folk of the day, such qualities being 'demanded by the higher branches of the work'!

Has anything changed, I wonder? An example of men working in the industry was quoted in this report, and it was no surprise to hear that Joseph Henson, another Pury End lacemaker, was Mrs Rogers' grandfather. Sadly, on the day before the article appeared, Mrs Rogers was taken ill. Hospitalized for a while, she died on Boxing Day (26 December) 1929, aged 65.

Mrs Clarke, herself a lacemaker as a child, remembers walking to Potterspury to deliver a nightdress case, hand edged in pillow lace, to the

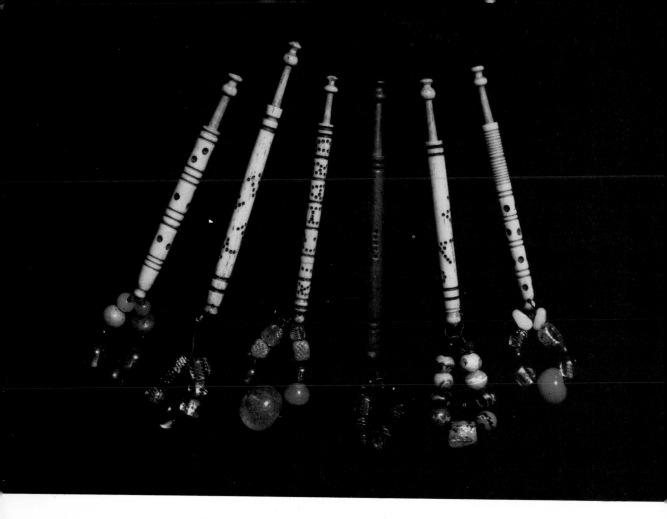

Compton bobbins from Deanshanger

home of Captain Holt. She was paid a guinea for the work, which she took home to her mother, that being the payment for two weeks' work, but in the declining days of the industry worse remuneration was known.

Payments of 2d a yard (a metre) for 5-inch-wide (13 cm) edgings and 6d for a collar were all they could raise when local outlets dried up and the lace had to be sent away. I was shown envelopes in which thread and orders were dispatched from the School of Stitchery and Lace, Vicarage Lane in Great Bookham, Surrey. Run by a Miss Sydney Smith, this school was in existence as late as 1940 and provided employment for sick and disabled young women, otherwise unable to earn their living. Another School of Stitchery and Lace based in de Montfort Square, Leicester operated in the same manner. They bought in lace and fine fabrics to make garments for ladies of fashion, who sponsored the schools or bought the clothes through postal catalogues issued by the Schools. This meant that even in the later years of a declining industry, the lacemakers whose interests had ceased to be served by a local industry could continue to earn a living at the pillow. Mrs Clarke, along with her mother and her sister, would make lace to order and send it off from the nearest Post Office, at Towcester. Mrs Clarke no longer makes lace, but her daughter, Mrs Allen, keeps the family tradition alive by attending classes locally.

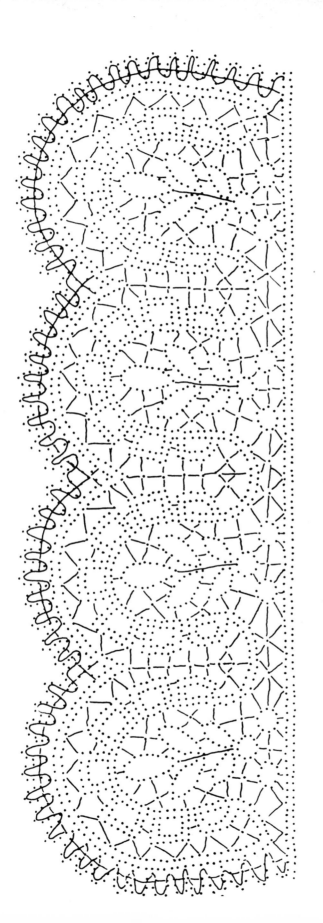

Pattern of a cuff. The
lace was made in Pury
End and purchased by
Queen Mary

Mrs Clarke's bobbins were made by her grandfather, and also locally at Deanshanger by the Compton family. Several of the latter turned up in Florence Varney's collection as well (*see* p. 77), so I decided they warranted investigation. The Compton family, father and son, made bobbins between 1858 and 1910 in the village of Deanshanger near Buckingham. A small village until the arrival of modern industry, its closest lacemaking neighbour was Wicken, whose lace was featured in the A.S. Cole report of 1893 on the Midland Lace Industry (commissioned by the Home Office). The bobbins have one outstanding characteristic: the large and well-formed script used to put names on the shaft. The writing is instantly recognizable and has been used, unusually, to inscribe both wood and bone bobbins. Those in Mrs Clarke's family read:

On bone:

> '*EMMA STEVENS BORN OCT 17 1861*'
> '*A PRESENT FROM A FRIEND OF MINE*'
> '*LOVE TELL YOUR TALE OF LOVE TO ME*'

and on wood:

> '*LOVE*'
> '*LOVE ME*'.

Others that I know of bear the names: Emmanual, Ann, Leah, Maria and Archer.

The cuff pattern included in this chapter is reproduced from the original vellum pricking lent to me by Mrs Clarke. It is such a beautiful pattern that I was not surprised to hear that the set made to that design had been bought by Queen Mary, who was a patroness of the Bookham School of Stitchery and Lace.

The late Mrs Clara Webb (born 29 January 1899) was a contemporary of Mrs Clarke, and lived in Long Row. Her mother, Eleanor Herbert, made Bedford lace on a large straw-stuffed pillow and Clara, having a memory for names, was able to list their old lacemaking neighbours in 'the Row'!

> *Mrs Herbert (Clara's mother) Rose and Liza Bignall (their next-door neighbours),*
> *Mrs Scott,*
> *Anne Brown (No. 2, The Row)*
> *Mrs Kingston (No. 5, The Row) (before her removal to Northampton),*
> *Maude Watson (Mrs Kingston's married sister),*
> *Mrs Atkins (a very old lady) whose address she did not know,*
> *Mrs Rogers, Mrs Clarke and Mrs Smart, who lived just along from The Row.*

Some of the patterns made in Pury End had names such as The Fan,

Running River and The Beehive, and it was quite common for the lacemakers to sit up very late at night working by the light of a flash lamp to get the required amounts made. Flash lamps were made of a variety of objects; bottles of water placed in front of oil lamps figured in the memories of the Long Row inhabitants, and I found that these recollections of times past opened up a window on the world as it used to be. I should like to extend a special thank you to Mrs Ivy Clarke, Mrs Clara Webb, and the lacemakers of Paulerspury and Pury End, for lending me the patterns, and for sharing their memories of the Lace Industry.

10 'TOMORROW, TOMORROW, TOMORROW . . .' (*Potterspury diary, Anon*)

Potterspury, although not as prominent as the villages I have already discussed, has a recognized history of lacemaking, with its own small industry managed by Mrs Chettle under the auspices of the Midland Lace Association. The village lies to the east of Watling Street, a few miles south of Paulerspury, and there is a history of connection between these two villages which demonstrates how different our lacemaking lives are now.

Nowadays, improved communications and the fact that our livelihoods don't depend on our lace, have led to the sharing of patterns and skills, although even up to the beginning of the twentieth century patterns were jealously guarded. In an old diary shown to me I found indications of how strong that protection was:

7 June, 1891
> '*Today I must sew my dress for it is no more than seven weeks to my marriage, though does seem like an age. Bella be hard put now to get those extra yards for Mrs Sharps order and all got to be in Northampton one week tomorrow*'

30 June, 1891
> '*I got 1s 6d for a yard of Essie's making yesterday. What a carry on there was when I went to see them, and get our room all cleaned. I didn't aught to sit with the girls and stick pins when I should be making all ready for the day, as if it ever took me six weeks to clean a room*'

3[?] July, 1891
> '*Aunt Pritchard gifted me a fine white sheet, but mother made me sit out here to hem it, for I am grown too gawkin' tall to be a sewing with the others, I heerd Essie, Bella and Maude, a giggling and a talking about me I suppose, I do wish I could work my pillow.*

(Here are some pages were spoilt and stuck together.)

19 July, 1891
> '*Tommorrow, tommorrow, tommorrow* [sic] . . . *Then I shall get my pillow back.*'

4 August, 1891
> '*We are back and all is well. Mother seems real tired, and Essie has been ill, though much recovered now. There are many orders now, I hope I can work soon. Tom's Aunt Clackmore was very kind to us and the sea*

when quite [quiet?] was lovely, but I was feared that Tom would drownd and could not like it much. Jinny and Mrs Scott said I could see my new pillow today, it is a good round one. Very hard and with a cushion for it [pin cushion?]. I long to work, but I must learn me a new lace, it being not so wide as ours back home it should be easy.'

9 August, 1891

'All is come to a sad pass now for my lovely Essie is dead. She looked so much better tho' weary that we thought her recovered but Mr Harrison says she was but raised to look better for our return. I begged a bobbin from her pillow for myself and Mother gave me two that she won from her work. I cannot use them without I mind my little sister. I told my Tom this night that if I have a girl I shall call her Essie and he gave me a paper of pins that he had bought for her thinking her ill, and he and I sat together talking of the fun we three had.'

Bobbin winder won by Mary Harrison's great-grandmother for the highest standards of lacemaking in Paulerspury

Nothing after that is legible, but it seems clear that the writer was being prevented from working her pillow close to her wedding day as she was to move to Paulerspury afterwards, and she may have been tempted to transfer the design that she had been making in Potterspury over to Paulerspury by memory. It may seem incredible to us that lace was protected like this, but in order to develop the speed that made lacemaking a commercial proposition (albeit transiently), it was desirable to restrict the lacemaker to making only one or two patterns, so that familiarity with the design soon built a speed that we could never hope to emulate.

RIGHT: Bucks Point insertion (courtesy of Mary Harrison)

FAR RIGHT: Potterspury lace made by Julia Woods of the Plantagenet Group

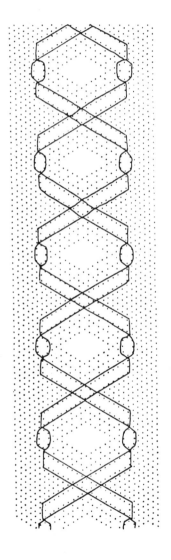

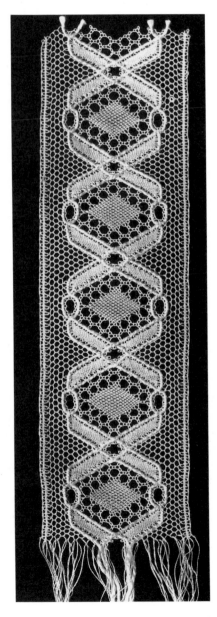

In attaining such high production speeds, however, it was inevitable that standards would vary, and many industries offered regular prizes as incentives for high-quality manufacture. Amongst the prizes offered by the Paulerspury Industry was a magnificent bobbin winder made by a Mr Paul of Towcester and presented as first prize to Mrs Cozzens of Paulerspury, for her work. The winder is now the property of Mary Harrison, her great-granddaughter.

Born in Paulerspury in June 1936 Mary lived at Spring Cottage, and recalls lace being made in the village even in those times. She remembers Rose Bignall and Mrs Clarke of Pury End making lace, as well as Ida Tomlin and the local shepherd's wife, even though they were then very old ladies. She was in a good position to know about the crafts of Paulerspury for her grandfather, William Marriott, had a haberdashery in Plum Park Lane and used to ride a penny-farthing bike around the villages selling penny pin-papers to the lacemakers. Her maternal grandfather bought the cottage in Potterspury where she now lives from the Duke of Grafton, and eventually the whole row came to belong to the family, several of whom were lacemakers. Her great-aunts made lace to order, and she has a number of patterns (not all of whose sources are known to her), some of which I have included in this book.

In Potterspury there is a row of cottages known as Factory Row, built by the Duke of Grafton to provide homes and a place of work for the poor of the village. One school of thought suggests that these cottages were originally designated for use as a lace factory; reliable evidence shows that they later became a match factory.

Madge Tapp, a resident of Potterspury (Church End), whom I taught until she emigrated to Australia in 1985, found an unusual collection of lace – not large but very interesting. In a packet about 8 × 11½ inches (21 × 30 cm) and bound in parchment were four sheets of parchment on to which were sewn strip after strip of lace. Each was at least six inches (15 cm) in length and, with one exception, there was only one design to the page. Each strip had been worked differently, as if producing a specimen of a particular method of working the pattern. I took the lace to Doreen Fudge at Luton Museum who expressed the opinion that the lace dated from approximately 1870 and that at least one of the designs was marketed through the BCWA and known as 'the Bow'. To Madge Tapp's great delight Doreen concurred with my opinion that this was a lacemaker's sample book, demonstrating different methods of working each of the patterns included.

It was common practice for small pieces of lace to be worked as samples, so that some choice of design could be offered to customers. One of the largest in existence is the Lace Dealers Sample Book held at Luton Museum, which includes many favourite designs in the intricate style of Lester, but our small sample book was, in its way, even more interesting than that, for it demonstrated the real grass roots of the lacemaking revival. Lacemakers seeking work within the new industries often had to supply

Factory Row in Potterspury

samples of the lace that they were used to working, and I believe that what Madge had uncovered was the work submitted to a scrutineer.

Several large houses dominate the area between Paulerspury and Potterspury; one, situated at Potterspury, was the scene of many lace transactions, for the lace of Paulerspury and Potterspury were often bought as gifts for visitors there. One previous owner of this house was Captain Holt, who regularly placed orders with the lacemakers for his wife's lace, and he was not alone in giving 'gentle charity' by placing orders with local women. Lace from this village was often sold abroad and at one time parcels of lace with a value of up to £10.00 are recorded as having been sent to America, although the local industry never achieved the regular turn of business abroad achieved by the BCWA.

I should like to leave this village with a memory of the look of astonishment on the faces of a group travelling with me on a guided tour of the Lace Villages. As our coach passed Factory Row they glimpsed, over the garden wall, a lacemaker at her cottage door working in the sunshine. Seated at a traditional pillow, with her winder at hand and a dog at her feet, Mary Harrison had been unable to resist demonstrating the view that had so attracted the Victorians. As they waved to each other and the cheers of enthusiasm came from my guests, for a minute the spirit of the lacemakers of times past was not far away.

11 THE BUCKINGHAM LACE INDUSTRY

The county town of Buckingham is in an area dominated by the lacemaking tradition. Its narrow market place is fronted by the old town gaol, and its streets are overlooked by the spire of Buckingham Church, crouched on the hill above the winding river valley on which the town is situated.

Buckingham's lace industry supported many dealers. In the seventeenth century Patrick Hanney, a bonelace merchant of Buckingham, is said to have travelled from door to door buying Point Ground; and in 1668 John Rennals, a lace buyer, issued his own 'trade token' with a strip of lace featured on one side.

Trade tokens were struck mainly by general merchants. Due to a shortage of small coins, caused by successive governments neglecting to mint enough, many traders were unable to offer change to their customers. Soon lacebuyers were also having to make their own 'brass farthings' in order to carry on trading. This practice, although unlawful, was carried out between 1648 and 1679, with surprisingly few cases of the issuing merchant failing to redeem their 'coin'.

Buckingham Church

Buckingham, The Royal and Ancient Borough (by D.J. Ellis) names several buyers and merchants: Thomas Ward (1755); John Bliss of Well Street (1842); and Mary Ann Clarke of North End.

Leisure-Hour notes on Historical Buckingham by J.T. Harrison (1909) mentions Mr Richard Viccars (one of Buckingham's last lace dealers) as 'requiring women to make a flounce which took 600 bobbins to work'! This book goes on to say that the flounce was worn by the last Duchess of Buckingham at her wedding and that her dress was preserved at Stowe. What eventually happened to it is unknown; the last Duke had no heir and Stowe was eventually sold; the contents of the house, including the fine library and documents, went to America, and the great house itself is now the famous public school.

Between Buckingham and Stowe is the village of Maids Moreton, and it is here that the revived Buckingham Lace Industry was established in 1893. Miss M. Burrowes, a talented and prodigious designer, ran this industry with formidable energy, paying particular interest to the standard of lacemaking demanded by her industry.

The Old Gaol in Buckingham

One method of raising standards amongst her workers was to get them to judge their materials with a critical eye, and she preferred them to ensure that their threads were:

> *obtained from the same [herself], for all orders given by the above. Too often inferior and mixed threads have been used which spoil the lace. The best and finest pins only must be used at Twopence three farthings a sheet, the commoner ones ruining the parchment.*

Miss Burrowes' motives were greatly misunderstood by the lacemakers, who accused her of trying to profit at both ends of the trade by her insistence on the use of good quality threads. In suggesting that her lacemakers should buy their thread from her, she intended to maintain control over only the quality of the lace but, of course, in a close community other motives were read into her actions. Although the industry in and around Buckingham, and as far away as Newport Pagnell, benefited from her advice, her delightful floral patterns, and her industry in promoting the use of Buckinghamshire lace, she was universally unpopular with the lacemakers themselves, who believed that her advice on thread was simply a device to profiteer at their expense.

Old Buckingham lace

Maids Moreton lace

By 1895 the number of workers in this industry had grown to 200, and besides the Duchesses of Buckingham, Sutherland, Buccleuch and Devonshire, the patronage of the Queen herself had been granted. Small wonder that the established Midland Lace Association approached Miss Burrowes to help organize the North Bucks Lace Association just starting up in Newport Pagnell, only 20 miles (30 km) away. She helped for a while, but it was obvious that no one person could run two lace industries simultaneously, and in 1902 she resigned from the Newport Industry saying that only by devoting herself to her own area could the efforts made by the lacemakers there be sustained.

Money was raised for both industries by the London Healtheries, a collection of exhibition shops set up to further interest in mind and body.

Successful lace exhibitions there in 1884 had been sponsored by the Duke of Buckingham and aroused great interest. The resulting orders on the books of two industries meant that the North Bucks Lace Association, in the capable hands of Mrs Carlysle, had enough funds for a paid Secretary, and the following notice was issued around the Lace Associations:

1876 Winslow Lace Industry (Bucks)	c/o the Hon Rose Hubbard
1883 Paulerspury Lace Industry	c/o Mrs Harrison
1891 Midland Lace Association	c/o President the Late Countess Spencer
1891 Potterspury Industry	c/o Mrs Chettle
1893 Buckingham Lace Industry	c/o Miss M Burrowes
1892 Thame Industry	c/o Miss Siverwright and others
1897 North Bucks Lace Association	c/o M Burrowes (Hon Sec) from 1897–1902 when resigned
1902 North Bucks Lace Association	c/o Miss Hewley

'The Buckingham Lace Industry was formed in 1893 to help the workers and revive the beautiful old Buckingham Lace, by Miss M Burrowes, this worked with unexpected success, and in the spring of 1897 in consequence of this, Mrs Carlisle asked Miss Burrowes if she would help her with the workers living around Newport Pagnell some 20 miles distant, and to try and form an association. This Miss Burrowes very gladly did and helped to form the North Bucks Lace Association, and acted as its Secretary temporarily for a few years, until she was able to leave it with ample funds to enable a paid Secretary to be kept. This was in 1902, when Miss Burrowes reverted to working her own Buckingham Lace Industry only again, as she had done since 1893. But owing to the amount of work required by both she could not combine to work both. In the autumn of 1902 Miss Burrowes wrote to Miss Knellys explaining that she had reverted to the working of her own industry only, and asking for the Queens Patronage on its behalf, 'as Her Majesty's kind interest is always such a stimulus and help to the workers'. Notices were also put in various papers stating that Miss M Burrowes had reverted to working her own district only again, so that it was hoped that no confusion would arise.'

As in all other lace villages, after the 1920s there was a rapid decline in industrial lacemaking. Workers leaving the industry discarded their pillows and bobbins, and many artefacts highly prized today, as much for their social history as anything else, were sold, given away and often burned, although thankfully many of Miss Burrowes' lovely floral designs, stamped with the legend 'Moreton Hall Industry' are to be found in the County Museum, Aylesbury.

Festival Catalogue with (below) details of Elsie Turnham's demonstrations at the North Buckinghamshire exhibition (part of the Festival of Britain, 1951)

Festival of Britain

NORTH BUCKS
EXHIBITION

Catalogue and Programme

TOWN HALL, BUCKINGHAM
SEPTEMBER 5th—18th, 1951
Open daily (Sundays excepted) from 3 p.m. to 8 p.m.

MISS ELSIE TURNHAM, who is a very well-known expert on Buckinghamshire lace, will attend the Exhibition on the following days : Wednesday, 5th September, Saturday, 8th, Tuesday 11th, Tuesday 18th. She will give demonstrations from 3.30 to 4.30 p.m. and from 6.30 p.m., followed by a talk at 8 p.m. on each of these days, and will be pleased to discuss the exhibits with visitors and answer their questions during the remainder of the time.

Skills were often passed on to children by the elderly lacemakers of the area, and in this way, Florence Varney and Elsie Turnham learned to make lace.

Miss Elsie Turnham, born at Waddesdon in 1885, demonstrated lacemaking at the North Bucks Exhibition, in the Town Hall at Buckingham. Part of the 1951 Festival of Britain, this exhibition was open to the public Monday to Saturday. Thousands of men, women and children flocked to see the exhibits and Elsie Turnham was kept extremely busy, demonstrating and speaking on several days of the exhibition.

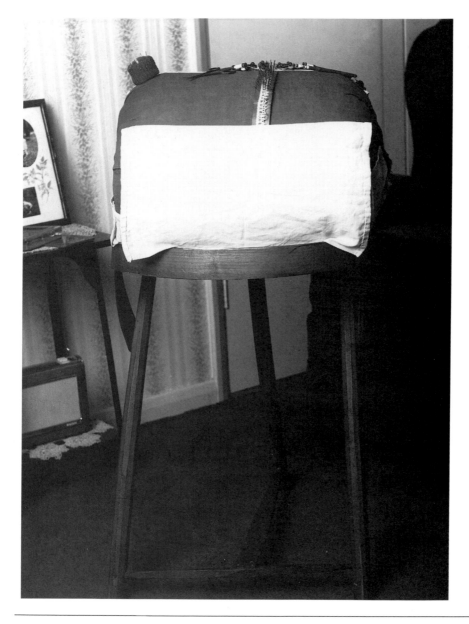

Pillow from Maids Moreton

Mrs Florence Varney's bone bobbins

Bobbins from Great Horwood

She had learned to make lace from one of the last professional lacemakers of her village and gained a name for collecting lace and bobbins, often buying up whole pillows discarded by the lacemakers as the trade died. When she died in 1956 her fabulous collection passed to her nieces, Mary and Diana Adams. Diana's tribute to her aunt's lacemaking life is entitled *Elsie Turnham; Lace Collector* (published by Kylin Press).

Florence Varney learned to make lace from Mrs Colton of Maids Moreton. Her pillow, an old-fashioned straw bolster supported on a pillow horse, came from a Mrs Stop of Maids Moreton. Her bobbins came from Great Horwood, from a Mrs Vine whose aunt had left them to her. With equipment from the Buckingham Industry (more than 100 years old when she received it) Florence Varney regularly makes narrow edgings and insertions for her grandchildren and great-grandchildren. Best of all, her granddaughter Gillian also makes lace, thus keeping up the family tradition.

Perhaps the last shop in Buckingham to deal in equipment for the professional lacemaker was run by the Misses Healey, in West Street. They also bought in finished lace to sell, and accepted commissions for the lacemakers, by 1938 dwindled to a precious few. Since the 1950s, however, lace supplies in Buckingham have ceased to be on open sale and it is hard to find any trace of the industry – lace or artefacts – in the antique shops today.

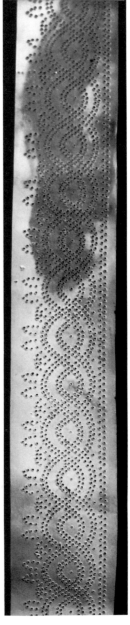

ABOVE: *Old Bedfordshire pattern on parchment, origin unknown*

LEFT: *Bucks Industry prickings, worn beyond use*

12 THE POOR VAUDOIS

Stony Stratford straddles Watling Street just south of the A508 road. In its original site Stratford held a strong strategic position at the ford across the River Ouse, which forms the county boundary between Buckinghamshire and Northamptonshire, but the town gradually split into two distinct parts: Old Stratford, on the Northampton bank of the river (even known as 'old' in the eleventh century) and Stony Stratford, south of the ford in Buckinghamshire.

A town of considerable importance, Stony Stratford had strong connections with royalty. The body of Queen Eleanor rested here in 1290 but the traditional 'Eleanor Cross' (believed to have been damaged during the Civil War) has since disappeared from its site at the north end of the town.

Watling Street was the main thoroughfare from Dover to Wroxester, and it was natural for travellers to seek overnight shelter in the town. Local traders did well from the travelling gentry and Stony Stratford became a sort of medieval 'services station', offering similar delights to those found in the modern day motorway equivalents.

Two royal visitors to Stony Stratford in the spring of 1483 were Edward V, aged 12 and his brother Richard of York, aged 10; accompanied by Sir Richard Grey, they were *en route* from Ludlow to the Coronation in London. That night, Edward and his retinue stayed in Stony Stratford at the Rose and Crown Inn while Sir Richard Grey travelled to Northampton to pay their respects to the King's Regent, Richard, Duke of Gloucester.

While travelling back to Stony Stratford with Gloucester's entourage (900 strong!) Grey was arrested. Seizing the opportunity to capture the King and his brother in the town, the Duke of Gloucester usurped the throne, becoming Richard III on 25 June 1483. In 1674 the skeletons of two children were found in a wooden chest near the White Tower. In 1933 post-mortem examination suggested that their ages would have been 13 and 10.

As was common in this area, agriculture was a major source of employment, with weavers and spinners well established in business with the nearby Priory at Bradwell. Tanning and sandal-making are mentioned

The former Rose and Crown Inn at Stony Stratford

Plaque commemorating the capture of the Little Princes in 1483

This house was anciently the Rose & Crown Inn & here in 1483 Richard, Duke of Gloucester (Richard III) captured the uncrowned boy King Edward V, who was later murdered in the Tower of London

in contemporary records, and in the seventeenth century lacemaking appeared and became the main trade of the town, after the hostelries.

Stony Stratford, clearly divided by its High Street, fell into two main parishes: Calverton on the west and Wolverton on the east. A link with the Huguenots first came to light in Calverton, which may explain how lacemaking came to be so firmly established there.

Many parishes in Bedfordshire and Buckinghamshire collected for the aid of refugee Protestants who had arrived in England. During the exodus of the Flemish refugees, people not only raised funds, but found homes and work for those who settled here. Newton Blossomville held collections for them and lacemakers are known to have settled in Cranfield, but Stony Stratford's involvement was unknown to me until Bernard Cavalot, a local historian, allowed me access to his collection. Details of collections for the 'Poor French Protestants' were found in an extremely rare offprint from *Records of Bucks*, Vol. IV, entitled 'Notes on Calverton Manor in the County of Buckingham'. These notes, written by Dudley George Cary Elwes, land agent to the Earl of Egmont, were dedicated to the Rev. W. Pitt Trevelyan, rector of Calverton. Elwes goes into great detail about the Parish collections, in particular those made for charitable purposes, even giving details of sums donated by individuals, for example:

A collection in the Parish of Calverton, upon the Brief for the poor French Protestants, May 25th 1686

	Li [£]	s.	d.
Madam Bennett...................	03	04	06
Mr. Carpender. Minister	02	00	00
Total collected in Parish		06	02	08

Collections for the Flemish refugees of the previous century are not recorded, so I could find no precedent for this action. However, similar collections are repeated throughout the records, such as:

Another for the relief of the Poor French Protestants, March 1687

Simon Bennett esq	02	00	00
Mr Carpender	01	00	00
Mr Rooker	00	02	00
Meadflower Nicholas	00	00	04

These entries occur after the Revocation of the Edict of Nantes in 1685 and demonstrate the enormous repercussions of that action throughout the worldwide Protestant congregation. The Edict of Nantes granted a measure of religious tolerance in an intolerant world still reverberating to the echoes of the Inquisition. Granted by Henry IV of Navarre in 1598, it created peace out of a chaos of religious war and persecution, and granted the Huguenots not only the right to worship, but to own property, and to defend that property. Objections to the development of separatism eventually led to the sacking of La Rochelle in 1628.

In the aftermath, many French Protestants were forced to recant their religion and, falsely advised that the Protestant religion was failing, Louis XIV withdrew the Edict. The resultant flood of refugees: skilled weavers, lacemakers and embroiderers, fled to England, Holland and Prussia.

The next entry in Mr Elwes's book seems to express the feelings aroused in England by the expulsion of the Huguenots. Note the use of a French regional name in the following statement:

> *A collection in the Parish of Calverton, April 16th 1699 for the poor Vaudois, being between 11 and 12,000 driven into banishment by Popish Caucery [sorcery?] and Superstition.*
>
> *Mr Carpender. Minister*   *01 00 00*
> *his 2 servants Francis Dobbe*
> *and Edw. Martin 6d apiece*   *00 01 00*

This at least states a reason for the collections, although without specifying the industry of the refugees or their whereabouts. It seems to refer to the mass exodus of the Huguenots that resulted in lacemakers bringing the techniques of the Lille area to England. On a less serious note, the above made me wonder what dire sin the two servants had committed to be made to donate most of their month's wages to a purely private collection administered by their employer!

The last entry of this type may explain how different laces came to be imported into the same geographical region: 'A collection for the poor distressed and persecuted Protestants of the Principality of Orange Feb 24 1703'. No amount is mentioned, but it is clear to see that there was an on-going commitment to help the Protestant refugees fleeing the Continent, whatever their nationality. It is possible that the appointment of the Duke of Buckingham to the French court encouraged these charities in neighbouring areas. Lacemaking, however, was established in Calverton.

Lace and Calverton Parish seem inextricably entwined, for in 1806 the Manor of Calverton (including the parish) was sold jointly to the Earl of Egmont and Mr Oliver of Stony Stratford. In 1797 Mr Oliver was described as a lace merchant, although he subsequently started a private bank in Stony Stratford. In the 1820s his banking interest had been taken over by his son, John Oliver, in partnership with yet another lace merchant, John York. Oliver and York went bankrupt in the 1840s and I found no further mention of their business ventures, although in a building close to the site of the original bank, a school known as York House School was started in 1890. That school moved in 1902 to a building now known as the 'York House Youth Centre', where Plantagenet Lacemakers used to meet. No-one has been able to confirm that John York and the school had any connections but stranger coincidences have been known.

13 A COCK AND BULL STORY

Lacemaking soon became a major industry in Stony Stratford and it was inevitable that the coaching inns should become involved. One has only to walk down the High Street to realize that thanks to latter-day coaching routes, Stony Stratford has an extraordinarily large number of inns, hotels and public houses in proportion to the expected needs of a small town. The two most famous are The Cock and The Bull which have stood almost side by side in the High Street since the fifteenth century; eventually, the rivalry between them became so great that the innkeepers employed men to advertise their establishments to the travelling public in the hope of

View through the coach entrance to the yard of the Cock Hotel

securing the other's trade. Their exaggerated stories of luxury were so unbelievable that one man, having endured them for a longish journey, is said to have cried out: 'No! Tell me no more Cock and Bull stories', which may be how that expression originated.

Several incidents concerning lacemaking and Stony Stratford occurred during and shortly after the Civil War. One document, which appeared in 1646 under the title *Mercurius Rusticus*, quotes from the diary of the Rector of Tyringham, Master Anthony, who suffered appalling mutilation at the hands of Parliamentary soldiers when he and his nephews were seized by the dragoons. When they had 'come neere to Stony Stratford' he states that a detachment of dragoons went into the town and:

> seized upon a poore Bone Lace man and a shoemaker, robbed them of what they had, and in the same manner sent them prisoners to Ailesbury.

I first came across a lacemaker of the Restoration period in Hyde and Markham's *History of Stony Stratford*. This contains a letter, dated 6 March 1664, in which Hannah Green wrote to her cousin that she had 'received an commission for sundry gentlemen of the area, from ye master of ye Cok inn' and that having received thread and bobbins from the master of the hostelry, she had 'gone straitway home and set my daughters and boys to work'. Later in the letter she mentions receiving 'an half guinea' for each piece of work!

What caught my attention was the amount being paid for the lace. The innkeeper would require a commission, as well as repayment for the advance of threads and bobbins, so the amount actually being charged for each item was at least double that half-guinea. It was unusual for bobbins to be 'advanced' and this must have been a special commission.

The Restoration brought many changes, one being that the sombre garb of the Protectorate era was being discarded, and gentlemen were returning to Court in more elaborate clothes; perhaps the lace made by Hannah Green was for the collars now favoured in the Carolean Court.

Nowhere in her letter does she mention making the lace herself – Sir Frank Markham calls her a lacemaker – but Hannah herself does not. She says that she 'set her daughters and boys to work'. These boys were probably employed by her for they did not appear to be her sons. She may have been Mistress of a lace school; she was certainly not a common lacemaker, for she could read and write well enough to convey an air of excitement throughout the letter. However, the commission was an event in her life which she could never have imagined people speculating over 300 years later.

Although the Cock Inn features most prominently in the lace history of Stony Stratford, other inns in town were also involved in the trade. The 'Rose and Leaf' was a pattern purchased regularly at the sign of the Bull, and buyers from London held sales on alternate Fridays at the old Rose and Crown Inn. There were local dealers and merchants too, although by 1710 the business of lace dealing in Stony Stratford may have been oversubscribed, for James Clinton, indentured to William Dennis, lace buyer of Stony Stratford, found his articles also bound him to learn 'the art of a barber and periwig maker'!

There were lace schools here too, one of which was on the High Street, and one unsubstantiated story about it tells how the lacemakers, wishing to sell their lace directly, asked for permission to bring their lace to the yard of the Cock Inn. The innkeeper agreed but stipulated that all sales were to be made before the passengers entered the inn. The story goes that a young lad, sent to watch for the dust sent up by approaching coaches, would have to run down the hill to alert the lacemakers. In turn they would gather up all they had for sale and try to beat the coach into the yard. This conjurs up an amusing picture but I cannot believe much lace was sold this way!

Stony Stratford has always been a law unto itself, the people of the town acceding not so much to the will of the Lord of the Manor as to the economic power generated by the coaching inns. This independent attitude spread into the lace trade, and even involved the clergy, for in 1701 the Rev. Richard Hatch recorded in the Parish Register 'an adventure' in lace being sent out to William Hatch of Virginia, whom I assume to have been a relative. The incredible amount of lace sent was 125 yards (114 metres) in various patterns, the whole value being £3 17s 11d! However, Richard Hatch died in 1703 without making further reference to this exploit.

In a first edition of Pigot's *Buckinghamshire* (1823) a list of lace dealers and buyers of Stony Stratford was as follows:

Loe John	*Dealer*	*West Side**
Lyons R.	*Lace Merchant*	*East Side*
Smith Rbt	*Lace Merchant*	*West Side*
York John	*Tanner & Lace Merchant*	*West Side*
Lever James	*Pin maker*	*West Side*

* refers to the Parish the trader had his premises in. West Side was Calverton Parish, East Side was Wolverton Parish.

The introduction to the directory of Stony Stratford in the 1831 edition of Pigot's *Buckinghamshire* includes the following statement:

> *Lace is the manufacture of this place, nearly all the lower class of females being engaged in its production.*

So, whenever I master a new pattern, before I give myself airs and graces for my undoubted brilliance I remind myself what a lower class sort of female I am!

By 1889 the lace trade was in recession, and the lacemakers were trying to find outlets for their own work. Mrs Elizabeth Elstone sat in the window of a shop in Oxford Street, perhaps to attract visitors to her shop on the corner of Horsefair Green. She made a wide range of patterns, and was chosen to make lace for the Exhibition of 1862. Her daughters are still remembered in the town, but I do not know whether they made lace, although they were most knowledgeable on the subject.

The brickwork shows the original entrance to Mrs Elstone's Lace Shop at Horsefair Green, Stony Stratford

The lace from villages in Northampton was often brought in to Mrs Elstone's shop. Clara Webb recalled walking in to Stratford from Pury End with her mother to sell the lace at Elstone's. Mrs Elstone would measure the lace 'by the stick' and then Clara and her mother would meet Mrs Webb's sister for tea before walking home to Pury.

The pin factories are beyond living memory now, but there were two in Stony Stratford, one behind Market Square and the other in the High Street. Both were owned by the Lever family, who employed a dozen men and boys making brass pins. These pins were nothing like as fine or well formed as those we use today; often they would have no head, and the lacemakers were forced to use their ingenuity to protect their fingers. Heads for the pins would be made from the seeds of goose-grass which were picked

An Edwardian lacemaker

*The W. I. lacemaking
club at Stony Stratford in
about 1940*

green and forced on to the top of the pin, shrinking and turning brown and
hard as they dried. Another method of making heads for the pins was that
of using a drop of sealing wax on the end.

By the 1930s only a few villagers were still interested in making lace.
The women of the town had found alternative employment with the growth
of technology. However, determined not to let the craft die, the Women's
Institute (WI) started a lacemaking club and I have included a picture of
the group circa 1940. The lady who kindly lent me the photograph, Mrs
Beatrice Aylott, is on the far left of the central row, and she well remembers
the work of that club. In the main she made Torchon and Bedfordshire
lace, although she confessed to never really progressing beyond the
'beginner' stage.

These ladies perpetuated the lacemaking craft, often teaching in their
own homes, so that Stony Stratford, that according to Osbourne's 'London
& Birmingham Railway Guide' 'has considerable traffic carried on; but the
only manufacture is that of bone lace', should not lose its reputation for
being a major lacemaking town.

Nowadays, Plantagenet Lacemakers meet on Wednesdays outside Stony
Stratford. However, we began there, and still think of ourselves as Stony
Stratford lacemakers. Lacedays are held, and visitors encouraged. A
full-time bobbinmaker, and some part-time bobbinmakers live in and
around the town (*see* Chapter 14).

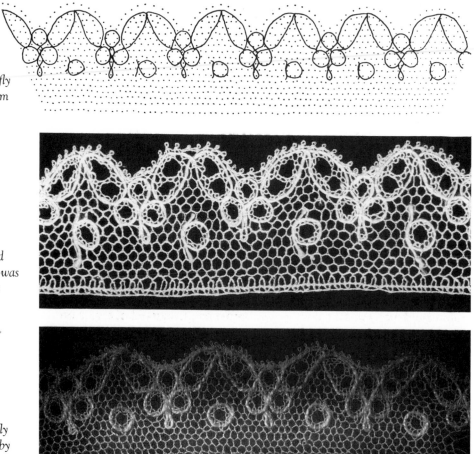

The Stratford Butterfly Pattern, redrawn from old lace

The original Stratford Butterfly. This piece was sold at Mrs Elstone's shop

The Stratford Butterfly redrawn and worked by the author using Mr Piper's 80 Poly-Cotton

14 OF RAILWAYS AND HANGINGS

In the early nineteenth century a new town with a huge railway works was built at Wolverton, and lacemaking was considered an activity with which the wives of the railway employees could suitably busy themselves. So New Towns are not just a modern imposition in this area!

Here there was an area of great potential for any dealer to tap. Goods could be transported easily, basic materials could be brought in comparitively cheaply, and in the surrounding villages there was a great need for work.

There was no reason to suspect that the railways would be anything other than good for the area. After all, as far as lacemaking was concerned, dealers had been travelling on lace-buying expeditions for years and the train would surely make things easier. Somehow, things did not work out quite the way they hoped.

Happy in the thought that traditional trades would benefit from a speeded-up form of transport, the authorities failed to notice that it was beyond human possibility to keep up with the demand that might ensue upon the opening of the transport frontiers. They did not foresee that the new technology would bring about the emergence of a faster, less aesthetically-aware society with a demand for practical clothing in step with this new pace of living.

Where lace was still in demand, speed of manufacture was more important than tradition. In addition, whole villages now sent their men and boys to work at the engineering works at Wolverton, and many women no longer needed to make lace for their livings. For those women who did need to work, the engineering works provided employment and, even if the sewing room was not glamorous, it provided a living for many of the girls of Wolverton and Stony Stratford.

Amongst the connections between the new railways and the old practices of the lacemaking villages lies one particularly gruesome incident – the first murder on a train. The murder itself was particularly horrible, and when I started to sort through the facts I had to keep reminding myself of the year in which it happened, for the events brought the developments in transport into prominence in a most disconcerting fashion. One Saturday evening in 1864 a bank clerk by the name of Thomas Briggs was returning to Hackney from Fenchurch Street Station on the 9.45 p.m. train. When the train arrived at the station a compartment was found to be covered in blood, and a subsequent search of the tracks found the clerk dreadfully injured and dying. He had been robbed of a gold watch and chain, and

*Changing modes of dress
at the end of the
nineteenth century*

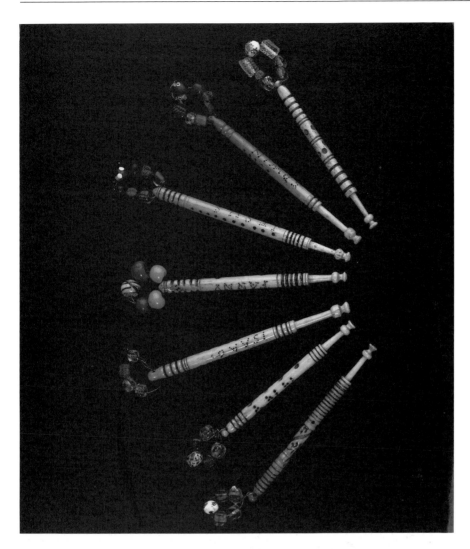

*Inscribed bone bobbins
(East Midlands style)*

callously flung on to the tracks; he died the following evening. On the following Monday, a jeweller in London contacted the police with a watch chain he wanted them to identify. He had exchanged the chain for a new one, at the request of a customer, and put the new one in a box which bore the name of his business. The police identified the chain as belonging to the murdered man, and a man-hunt was launched. The jeweller's box, meanwhile, had attracted the attention of a man whose child had been playing with it. The father, having read the reports of the murder, recognized the name of the jeweller inside the box, and promptly handed it in to the police, together with the description of the wanted man and his address. The net was closing in on Franz Muller, who had embarked on a sailing ship bound for New York. The police were forced to pursue him in a modern steam ship. They caught him and returned him to London, where he confessed his guilt just before he was hanged.

'Franz Muller hung 1864' is the commemoration seen on a lace bobbin, one of only six known hangings to be commemorated in this way. It is arguably one of the most significant of the hanging bobbins, for it records several 'firsts': the first murder committed on a train, the first foreign name to be inscribed on a hanging bobbin, and probably the first murderer ever caught by such a combination of transports. Incidentally, it was this murder that led to the installation of an emergency signal that passengers could use in the event of trouble.

The author

Of course, new technology did not put an end to the days of gracious dress and the wearing of lace, but it had a lot to do with its decline. However, lace has always been treasured, and even if you could not use it you certainly did not throw it away, and so it has survived, tucked away in drawers and boxes, handed on from mother to daughter, grandmother to grandchild . . . and I amongst many others have benefited from this. Some items in my collection have always generated interest at lacedays and I include some photographs for you here.

Baby's cap (author's collection)

Youghall needlepoint collar (author's collection)

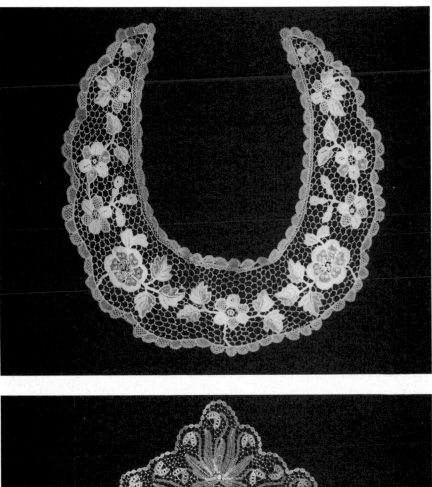

Branscombe handkerchief (author's collection)

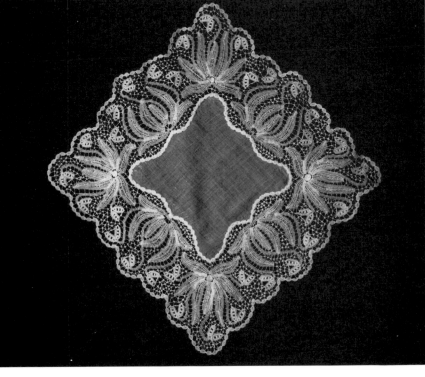

FAR RIGHT AND OVERLEAF: Point d'Angleterre, probably of the seventeenth century (author's collection)

*Black cap and lappetts,
bought by the author
from a local market stall!*

*Bedford collar (made
from strips of antique lace
to the author's design)*

*Tape collar with
needlepoint fillings,
Victorian*

*Simple but effective
Bedford Tray corner,
possibly BCWA*

Honiton Bertha

Detail of parasol, note the three differing 'rings' effect (see p. 18*)*

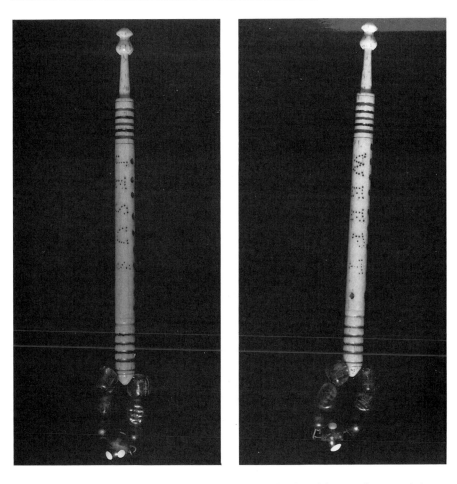

My favourite bobbin. Made by Bobbin Brown and inscribed 'Jesus Weept', believed to have been an Easter gift

I have been helped greatly in my research by local lacemakers and the following may serve to give an impression of what is going on in Lace Villages today.

Sherington Lace Group has been in existence for more than three years, starting in the summer of 1986. The founding members, Josie Sears and Jenny Hicks, felt the need for a more local group than those in existence in Olney and Newport Pagnell. After having contacted all the lacemakers that they knew by telephone, and putting up some notices, they held a meeting at Josie's house and were astonished when ten people, mainly beginners, turned up. Since then the group has grown and now meets at the Sherington First School on Monday evenings with about 20 members. They think of themselves as a village-based self-help group, they hold workshops from time to time, and have a 'Pillow and Chat' evening once a year in the village hall. Josie Sears is a well-known supplier of lacemaking equipment and, as a founder member of the group, would be very happy to correspond with anyone with similar interests. In particular, Sherington Lacemakers would be pleased to hear from anyone who knows anything of the lacemaking background of the village. (*See* p. 136 for their address.)

The Sherington Young Lacemakers was established as a separate group at the local school in 1983. This was started by Mrs Mary Russell, headmistress of the school at the time, and has approximately 18 members. Now taught by Mrs Barbara Barnwell, the Young Lacemakers allow pupils from other schools to attend their group.

Sherington Lace Group today

Founder members of the Sherington Lace Group

The Plantagenet Lacemakers are comparative newcomers to Stony Stratford and were created by joining together members of a private class with students from Further Education classes. Started in September 1988, the group is composed of about 30 lacemakers of varied experience, and meets twice a week. Serious classwork is carried out in our morning meetings, with gossip and experimental work in the evenings. We have had one very successful lace day, at which Veronica Sorenson was a delightful and informative speaker, and we plan more for the future.

LEFT: *Claire, our special member, enjoys her tea as much as her lace!*

BELOW: *Plantagenet lacemakers*

15 MIXED LACE

Some readers may have old patterns pricked on skin or parchment, and it may be useful to explain here how to look after them, whether you can work on the old parchments, and how to reproduce them if the original is unworkable in its present state. For this information I am most grateful to Mr Vischer, of Cowley's Vellum Manufacturers, who suggested that I try my hand at actually using parchment to make a pricking and to comment on its properties. It was an experiment well worth the effort.

Parchment comes in many thicknesses and you should tell the manufacturer for what purpose you require the skin before purchase. The best, to my mind, is almost transparent (makes pricking from a photocopy very easy) and fairly flexible. Use the parchment in your usual fashion, but make sure you start with a new needle in your pricker. The material pricks with ease, much better than card. You will have no trouble passing your needle through the skin and I found that there was no need to 'wax the needle'. Parchment *is* very expensive, so do not want to waste it on everyday patterns but if you want a permanent record of a special pattern it is ideal material.

I also received some tips on preserving old skin prickings:

1 Keep your parchments dry, but not overly hot (they don't like central heating).

2 Many old parchments roll up, and in order to 'relax' the skin to correct this you will need to keep the pricking in a totally unheated room (such as a garage or cold utility room) for a night. Allow the skin access to the cold night air, and in the morning you will be able to correct the coiling of the parchment.

Do this slowly, reversing the roll by supporting the parchment on a cardboard tube. The diameter of the tube should be no less than 1½ in. (38 mm) and you may find it easier to use if you cut a slit in the tube the width of the pricking, and slip just enough of the parchment inside that slit to secure the end of the pricking. Carefully roll the pricking on to the roll in the opposite direction to the one in which it was previously coiled, and then secure it by tying a little string or wool about it. In an astonishingly short period of time, your pricking will straighten.

3 If the pricking is so long as to make it impracticable to keep flat, then remember to wrap the pricking around a cardboard tube, as previously described, to prevent excess pressure from cracking the parchment.

Old parchments in good condition are hard to come by, and it is advisable not to work on them directly. You may have parchment and card prickings that have already cracked, or that have become so darkened or damaged by time as to render them unusable. The method described below is one familiar to architects – the dyeline process.

This process, available in many photocopying and printing agencies, is designed to produce the 'negative' from which blueprints are made. The basic idea is that any area not permeated by light goes black and areas that let light through (such as pin holes) remain white. The resulting print taken from your old prickings will be black with white dots; semi-transparent parchments may show gimp lines, or the inked indications of leaves and plaits. If you trace the dots, adding any drawn details, copying by eye from the original parchment, you should then be able to tell whether the pattern is worth spending much time on.

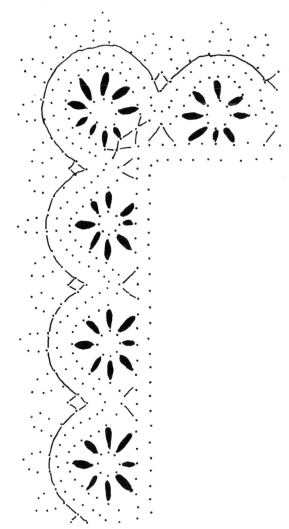

A simple but effective corner pattern

I would emphasize that whether or not your prickings are suitable for this process depends entirely on the state of the actual pricking, and the nerves of the dyeline operator. You may ruin your pricking if it is not in suitable condition. If the card is torn or flaking you should seek advice first. Again, the best results are not obtained unless the machine is going comparatively slowly, and the pattern has been used. Patterns that have never been used often have small pin holes that may not let the light through.

Finally, remember that if you decide to go ahead and dyeline your prickings, the dyeline print will fade and eventually disappear altogether if exposed to light. Trace the pin holes by hand as soon as you can, and then work out the extras later, using your original pricking.

William Haycock's grandmother, known as Polly

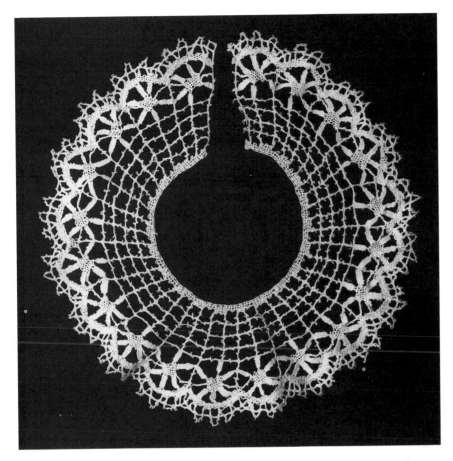

*One of Polly's pieces
(courtesy of
W. Haycock)*

Whilst I was in Olney I made the acquaintance of William Thomas Haycock, a gentle man with many memories of lacemaking times. He was born on 10 May 1903 in Braefield, and lived his early years in the village of Hackleton with his 13 brothers and sisters. His grandmother was a professional lacemaker, known variously as 'Aunt Polly' and 'Mary' and Mr Haycock remembers her making lace by the light of an oil lamp that had been fitted with an older flash bulb and something that he remembers being called a taper cone, which I think might refer to the practice of shielding the reflective bulb with a cone of brown paper.

She was certainly a homeworker, and he recalls her lace being sent down to Armstrongs at the Lace Factory. She was a Baptist by religion, strong in her family commitments, and a vigorous, spirited lady. One event that obviously brings back happy memories of childhood delights was the excursion to the bakehouse on Sundays to get the meals cooked. William remembers family squabbles over who should take the meat to be warmed.

He did not know what had happened to his grandmother's lacemaking equipment, although it is possible that his mother, Minnie Elizabeth, may have had some items, as she was an amateur lacemaker of some kind.

*A Bedford lace pattern
given to the author in
Towcester*

William remembered that his grandmother could not read or write and depended on lacemaking to make her living. She had an invalid husband to nurse, in which duty she took great pride. He had been involved in a bombing incident in 1916 and afterwards was unable to walk or earn a living, but Mary managed on a pittance and always kept him spotlessly clean and happy.

Bedford corner, which may have come from Newport Pagnell

Her linen lacemaking thread came from Olney and was supplied by Armstrong's, later from Sowmans ironmongers. This demonstrates that even without the support of the Agency, lacemakers were making enough lace to encourage local supplies of ordinary goods. William's last memory of his grandmother is her walking to visit her married daughter, draped in her customary shawl.

The young gentleman featured in scout uniform was another whose story I simply had to tell: Dick Hayles, from Bedford, kindly allowed me to talk to him of his lacemaking memories. His was a childhood of scouting in the early days of the movement and where holidays meant horse and cart journeys to catch the train to the sea. He got his pillow from his sister, after she went into service, and was taught to make 'Old Point' by a neighbour, later demonstrating his skills in the Ideal Home Exhibition held at Olympia. His scout group held stand Number 26 and, not far from their demonstration, E.P. Rose and Son of High Street, Bedford were offering their lacemaking goods, including Torchon Roller pillows at 7s 6d each! He still remembers how to make the 'Little Fan' and is a most courteous and charming man who was a privilege to meet.

Dick Hayles

16 BEDFORDSHIRE LACE

Bedford is a large town, encircled by modern estates and the inevitable growth of industrial activities. The older parts of the town, however, particularly those around the Embankment, are largely unspoilt and exist in an atmosphere of enviable serenity. There, large houses of the Victorian era look across the River Ouse, bringing back memories of a gracious age when the gentlewomen of the town would purchase their veils and lappetts from T. Lester and Sons in the High Street.

Several lace dealerships existed in the town and in the nineteenth century, the Lesters were to come to prominence in this field, employing many of the women in the local villages in the manufacture of traditional Bedfordshire lace. After the Great Exhibition of 1851 they busied themselves with design innovations, and the lace that resulted won national approval and several awards for Lester. This came at a time when designs for bobbin lace were at low ebb, and did much to restore the fortunes of Bedfordshire lacemaking.

Thomas Lester entered the trade at a time when the amount of foreign lace being imported had fallen. The late-eighteenth-century conflict with France had reduced imports from Continental sources and, during this time, English lacemakers enjoyed an unrivalled prosperity. In spite of this happy interlude, when manufacturers were able to encourage both improved standards and the introduction of more complicated designs, the Industrial era was just beginning and, in the north Midlands, the invention of the lacemaking machine seemed certain to stunt the growth of the traditional craft. Lacemaking, however, was certainly the principal trade of many Bedfordshire villages and the lace manufacturers of the times could not afford to give up too easily.

Bedfordshire had, at its source, the same settlers as those of Buckinghamshire and Northampton, but when Lester took up lace dealing in the early nineteenth century the origins of the craft had been almost forgotten. Huguenot names had been absorbed into the Directories of the countryside (these listed the names and occupations of local people), and if a Perrin lived here or a Gerard there, there were many more lacemakers in the valley of the Ouse whose origins were quite English!

Known as 'Old Point', Bedford lace at that time used the same wire ground and many of the patterns of Lille lace, which gained huge popularity with the fashionable because the delicacy and filmy nature of the narrow edgings and insertions made them perfect foils for the gossamer fabrics and fine lawns of the period. However, the work was extremely slow, with many dealers bewailing the time taken between the issue of the design and the return of the work.

Because of the demand for bobbin lace, by 1800 the industry relied not only on large numbers of village women in the surrounds of Bedford, but also on most of their children, who were put to lacemaking almost as soon as they could walk. Lacemaking was particularly suitable for their employment because it required 'little in the way of muscular strength or size' (Thomas Lester). The lacemen, many of whom were itinerant, were thus able to take many differing laces to London on a regular basis, and often designed their own patterns which were then worked by lacemakers in 'their own industry' (Thomas Lester), but changes were afoot!

At the turn of the nineteenth century a twisted net was perfected by the machine-lace entrepreneurs of the Midlands. This was quickly taken up by the Honiton workers, who used it to sew their sprigs on, thus forming a lighter and more speedily worked lace. In addition, this method was less labour intensive than the old practice of joining motifs with bobbin net. Soon other lace manufacturers, including Lester, followed suit, using this net to produce 'falls', or veils, and bonnet veils, by joining hand-made lace to the sheer net. This allowed widths of lace to be produced in regional areas where the traditional laces were confined to narrow edgings and insertions. However, this was not enough for the Nottinghamshire engineers who were still hard at work trying to replace traditional lacemaking methods. When, in 1840, a true machine 'lace' was produced, the battle for survival began.

Ironically, the machine laces copied faithfully the designs of the Midlands, and although the inventors' technical skill was much admired by the Victorians and a great fashion in machine laces was predicted, such admiration could scarcely have been echoed by the bobbin lace dealers who were now facing disaster.

Previously, imports had been the lace merchant's worst enemy. Periods of free trade had allowed foreign laces into the country, often at prices that undercut national products. Protests from manufacturers and suppliers of lace won a short-lived ban on all imports in 1699, but that Act and the difficulties in enforcing it, were unlikely to be repeated in the nineteenth century. During that early prohibition lace, already on the list of desirable objects to smuggle, started to enter the country in much larger amounts. Before long it was necessary to devise some way of sending large bales of lace into the ports of England in such a way that the Customs and Excise would be completely unable to detect it, and the result of this was the distasteful practice of concealing large amounts of lace in the coffins of travellers who had died abroad. Obviously it would have been impossible to arrange for the examination of every coffin entering the country, and no doubt there were genuine cases where the deceased person had made a request to be buried in his own country, but a sudden large increase in these incidences attracted the attention of the authorities, who soon discovered that not every coffin contained a body, nor in fact had ever been intended for that purpose.

FAR RIGHT: *Narrow laces, typical of the pre-1880s Bedford villages. Many rescued and in bad condition*

Despite hindrance from groups of mourning 'relatives', the Excise men made several large finds; one report concerned the deceased Bishop Atterbury, whose body had been returned for burial in Westminster Cathedral after his death in 1731. The High Sheriff of Westminster must have been exceedingly gratified with his search of the coffin (which in itself must have been quite a controversial occurrence – if the story is to be believed) for he recovered some £6,000-worth of lace!

The subsequent increase in searches demonstrates that the authorities would brook no argument with grieving relatives, no matter how exalted a rank the deceased had held in life. Much later, in 1764, the Duke of Devonshire died abroad, and despite family protests his coffin was searched for lace – abortively as it turned out – but this determination of the Customs and Excise officers was soon to manifest itself in an abrupt decline in the number of deaths abroad!

Despite all this, a genuine desire for Continental lace and better relationships with the lace-producing countries re-established the trade, this time with a sliding scale of taxation, dependent on the width of the lace, to protect our own lace industry. With the greatest tax being levied on the narrowest laces, for a while it was cheaper for those seeking narrow edgings to use English lace. Thus from 1806 to 1815 the industry in the Midlands was cushioned against competition. However, even before the war with France was ended, a proposal to extract a simple block levy of only 20 per cent, against all widths of imported lace, was put forward, and it took the combined efforts of the merchants up until 1819 to get that proposal squashed. Again, the protection of trade afforded by such taxation was minimal, as the foreign imports still held much attraction for the ladies of the nineteenth century.

The fact that Queen Adelaide herself seemed to favour the very popular blonde silk bobbin lace from France did not escape the eye of the local industry who, together with the neighbouring lace areas of Bucks and Northampton, felt it unfair that they were being subjected to further incursions of foreign lace when traditional English lace had as much to offer.

Blonde lace was very much in demand for evening wear, and had the added attraction of also being available in cream and black. Despite the fact that the lacemaking method was the same, very little was produced in the Midlands, the industry there wishing to maintain its own traditions; so the lacemakers of three counties, forced to watch the fashionable import worn by many nobles and Court figures, eventually approached the Duke of Buckingham who was known to be favourably disposed to their cause. With his help, they petitioned Queen Adelaide to wear the white lace of the Bedford industry, and they were promised the assistance that they sought – but it has to be said that, even with such exalted help, much had to be done to put Bedfordshire lace back into full heart.

The local industries still clung to outdated business methods. The lace merchants, also known as lace buyers, or lacemen, controlled the

OVERLEAF
LEFT: *Narrow Bedfordshire edgings worked in very fine linen. From the village of Houghton Conquest*

RIGHT: *Shaped pieces of the newer Bedford/ Maltese style of lace, made in Wootton, when standards of lacemaking were declining*

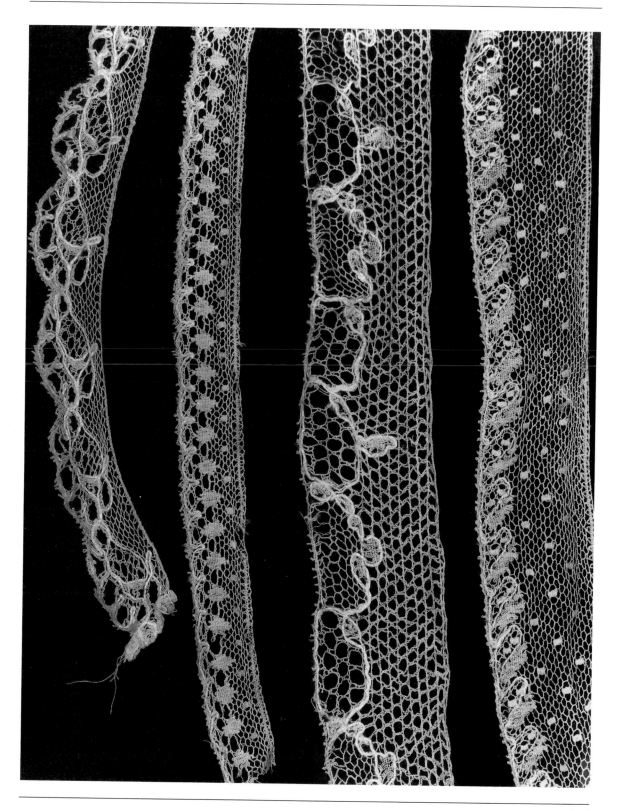

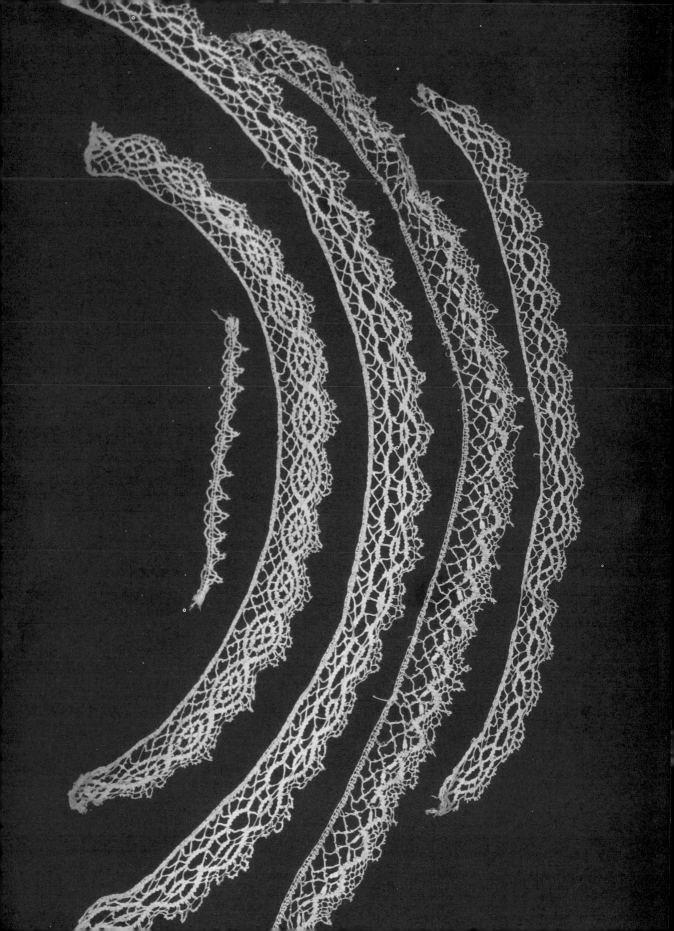

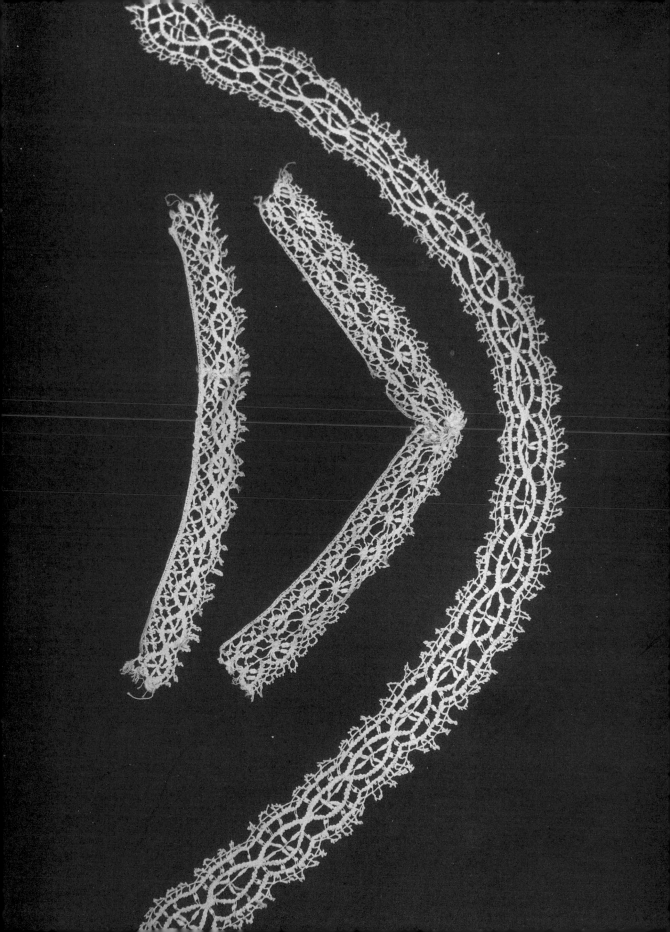

A piece of lace obviously inspired by some of the Honiton fillings, rescued from a dress consigned to a jumble sale!

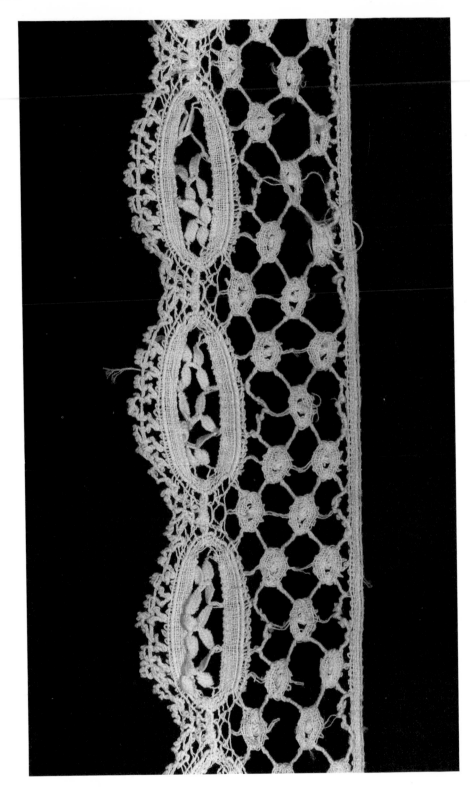

distribution of patterns and often the purchase of threads. Many shared a lacemaking area, with no absolute control over the lacemakers of their industries; lacemakers preferring to work for several dealers rather than pinning their fortunes on one. This lack of organization helped to produce yet more complication within the industry, and left many of the dealers doubting the loyalty of the workers. Strictly speaking, although a lacemaker was not bound to any one merchant, it was a point of honour that finished lace should be returned to the merchant who had supplied the pattern. Designs, however, were worth money and in some cases lace made to one merchant's pattern would be sold to another, that piece of lace being all a designer would need to adapt the pattern so that he could call it his own. This practice became so rampant as to produce a general call amongst the designers, not least of whom was James Millward of Olney, for a registry of lace designs. Strangely, the name Lester never appeared on that registry, although the father, Thomas Snr, and the son, Thomas Jnr, are widely believed to have been the foremost designers of their time.

Between 1800 and 1840 vigorous attempts were made to introduce education for all children. Throughout the nineteenth century various reports were compiled with regard to the employment of children in various traditional crafts and, in Bedfordshire, the crafts that received the closest attention were straw plaiting and lacemaking. In 1863 a report on the findings of J.E. White appeared, and although a great proportion of that report had to do with the emergent machine-lace trade, he spoke of one dealer in Bedford employing 3,000 people, which suggests that he was, in fact, referring to Thomas Lester. Lester himself contributed to these reports, that were eventually used in setting up the Elementary Education Act (1872), which compelled parents to send their children to school. Lester, who at that time had already been 50 years in the trade, spoke about the wide area from which the lacemakers of his industry were drawn. His workers came from all of the villages within a ten-mile radius of Bedford town itself, and also from Buckinghamshire and the county borders of Oxfordshire; an extraordinarily large catchment area, giving some picture of how many hands were required to keep the Bedford industry alive. Of course, it was not possible for Lester to see all his lacemakers personally, and he delegated much of the delivery of new designs and the collection of the lace to other small buyers with whom he had business dealings. It may well be that some of the many designs that exist 'after the style of Lester' were copied in transit – the need for new designs being one of paramount importance.

During the eighteenth century, in Bedfordshire, whole industries based on lace made in the workhouses came into existence. Records dating from 1719 show that pauper children, dependent on the workhouse, were taught to make lace at Eaton Socon, St Paul's Bedford and as late as 1801 from Bedford Gaol itself. Even the poorest and the least educated were sufficiently skilled to operate within the industry. The words of the French jurors at the Paris Exhibition of 1867 declared: 'The English lacemakers are

Thomas Lester of Bedford (by kind permission of the Trustees, the Cecil Higgins Art Gallery, Bedford)

skilled, work thread and silk easily and produce work of excellent quality'.

However skilled the work was perceived to be, somehow that skill was never attributed to the lacemaker except in the rarest of cases. Somehow, the consumer managed to attribute the beauty of the developing lace of Bedford to the designer, completely overlooking the fact that the designer's idea was a long way from the completed lace until interpreted by the lacemaker. Many are the instances of Bedfordshire children being called stupid, dull, lackwitted and backward when they entered into regular education, but never was any attention paid to the fact that many of these laceworkers worked ten hours a day at the pillow and could therefore only attend school on a half-time basis.

In the case of the emerging Bedford/Maltese and the Lester laces of the period, it was particularly outrageous that little attention was paid to the fact that lacemakers were expected to review their traditional methods and adapt to those required to create the new designs, without any loss of quality. To adapt to a new discipline is hard enough, but to do it in a working context, without loss in standards or volume of production, seems to me to be especially admirable.

During the early industrial era, many fortunes were made by the new business barons; however, for the traditional dealers and buyers, the fortunes made were easily outnumbered by fortunes lost – and not all because of the changes in trade. Back at the beginning of the changes in the Bedfordshire lace industry, in the period between 1800 and 1840, many buyers facing the competition of the merchanized industry, simply gave up, but others went out of business for more prosaic reasons, and in the course of research I came across a document that chronicles one such event.

Amongst the dealers engaged in the lace trade in the Bedford locality were John Claydon, described as a lace dealer, and Thomas Collier, described as a lace merchant, both from the village of Sharnbrook, from where it is said that the best wooden bobbins of the period came. Collier and Claydon set about becoming partners on 1 July 1820, with disastrous results for both of them. The documents that I have found relate to the dissolution of their partnership, and I thought that it would be interesting to show that there is no proprietary right to business rogues in this century!

Apparently, on instituting their partnership, they limited the time that that partnership should trade for to 'not less than 1 year and not more than 3 years' and they further agreed to an equal share in profit and loss, with a 5 per cent return for either partner advancing capital beyond the property left by John and Robert Talbot, whose trade at Sharnbrook they had taken over.

The property and effects of the trade run by the Talbots, including threads, laces, gimps, horse and gig etc., were valued and added to loans (made by the Talbots) to the new partners; an amount of £3,000 was arrived at, and a bond dated 1 January 1821 was executed on Collier and Claydon in respect of that sum.

Collier himself added a further capital sum of £700 to the business, but it seems that Claydon put forward nothing. They commenced trading, and before long the Talbots were having to make other loans; in total they were soon owed the sum of £3,400. That this situation could not continue was soon obvious, and when a valuation was applied to the trade it was discovered that although a stock of £2,000 existed, monies due to the Talbots amounted to £3,400. After disbursements and sundry small debts Collier and Claydon could not afford to continue.

A full examination of the accounts revealed that John Claydon had 'applied £1,700 to his own use, and is unable to make up the deficiency'. On 5 January 1822 the partnership was dissolved, the stock being given to Thomas Collier, who also received Claydon's cottage (value £200) and his chattels, as some compensation for his losses. However the document of dissolution went on to say that the deed in no way discharged Claydon from his liabilities, which still amounted to £1,100, less the sum raised on his property and chattels.

Many such debtors were sent to the Fleet prison, and some research carried out into this infamous prison revealed that a great many of its inhabitants were those who had been engaged in poorly paid work. The majority of those convicted of actual crime were male labourers, but a close second was run by women, employed either as servants or in some capacity within the textile trades. There was a mantua-maker, several milliners, glove-makers, tambour workers and even two lacemakers: Lucy Brand, aged 33, sentenced at the Old Bailey for larceny, and Maria Hamilton, a lace weaver, sentenced to the Fleet for the theft of apparel at the Old Bailey. Of course, it is not fair to insinuate that dishonesty of any kind could be attributed uniquely to certain craftworkers, or even classes of person, but it does seem that driven by poverty and desperation, crime may have seemed the only way to keep body and soul together, as the lace trade entered the worst period of recession it had ever known.

17 THE EVIDENCE OF THE CHILDREN

During the early nineteenth century the situation regarding child labour had attracted the Government's attention, and active steps were taken in many traditional areas of employment to ensure that children employed in workshops had access to true education, and that the conditions they were forced to work in were not dangerous or detrimental to their health. Several commissions were set up to explore the needs of the children, and in the years running up to the passing of the Elementary Education Act, these commissions sought evidence from many sources. They had very few powers themselves, but served to make recommendations on child labour to the Government, which in turn took a series of steps to protect the interests of working children prior to the passing of the Education Act.

Early steps in educational reform included the setting up of schools largely adherent to one or another religious denomination, but there were many children whose parents could not afford to send their children to what were then fee-paying schools. These children had little access to education and in this group were many of those involved in the lace industry. Evidence from the organizers and/or owners of lace schools, the major dealers, and even the children themselves, was called forward, and every aspect, from the sizes of rooms that the schools were held in, to the age groups of children and the hours worked, was examined. Inspectors visited schools and tested the children's ability to read, add up and their general level of awareness of life outside the village.

In the main, the educational level was appallingly low, and one senses the despair of the Inspector who, on visiting the Houghton Conquest lace school, discovered at least one child who did not know what the word 'sea' meant. Sadly, it is not to be supposed that there were many differences between the children of any of the three lacemaking counties that we have examined.

In 1818 lace was specifically mentioned as 'adversely affecting the progress of education' – it is little wonder. The villagers could see no benefit in learning about a wider world than they would ever experience, and preferred either to send their children to the local lace school in order for them to earn their keep, or to teach them at home to work alongside their mother at the pillow. You have already read how whole villages depended on the difference that lacemaking made to the family income, and how jealously guarded were the patterns of Buckinghamshire and Northamptonshire. It cannot have been all that different for the villagers of such places as Marston Moretaine, and Wootton, to name but two of the many villages on the fringe of Bedford, whose names have come to be synonymous with the Bedford lace industry.

In Marston Moretaine there were, in fact, nine lace schools at one time, which seems today an excessive number and may have seemed so even then, but of course, the lace schools were nothing like schools of today. They often consisted of a single room, with little or no attention paid to the children's comfort, and with no facilities for heating or exercise; it is a miracle that more children did not succumb to the hazards of their surroundings. Some of the schools attempted to teach the children to read 'albeit very imperfectly' (Bedford Schools Inspector's Report, 1862) but most relied on day or evening schools for any training in matters not connected with the lace trade. The children attended these schools from an early age, and a description of Mrs Burnidge's Lace School at Houghton Conquest as late as 1865 may suffice to give a picture of the conditions.

The school was run in a room 11ft 6in (3.5m) by 11ft 9in (3.6m) and at the time of the report Mrs Burnidge was used to having 24 children, herself and two 'sitters' in the one room, working! The fireplace was not used, so that the room could accommodate this number of people, and instead a counterpane was fixed over the fireplace 'to keep out the draught'. In this confined atmosphere girls came to make lace from the age of seven, leaving when they were about 13 or 14 (employable age). The hours were long, from 8 a.m. until 5.30 p.m. or later, with a half day on Saturday and Sunday off. Mrs Burnidge herself thought that the children in her care could read and write, most of them going to Sunday School. She commented that very few girls attended the evening school that existed at the time, although the boys went. Mrs Burnidge charged a fee of 2d a week, and the children were expected to earn from 1s to 2s 6d a week with their work, although little was earned by the youngest children. Mrs Burnidge made herself responsible for the sale of the work produced, differing from some of the other local schools that expected the children to go into Bedford to sell their own work!

The conditions at the Elstow school seem to have been rather better, with a new room being built to accommodate the lacemakers at the time of the report. Many of the women of Elstow were lacemakers and, besides the lace school run by Mrs Goodman, there was a good day school that taught sewing, reading and sums for 2d a week. Mrs Goodman, on being examined by the visiting inspector, thought that most of the children in attendance could read and write, and commented that, in the main, the older girls and women worked alone in their own houses and not in sets at each other's homes. In doing so she seems to confirm that there were two recognized practices amongst the lacemaking communities within her knowledge. She also seems to have been favourably disposed to the 'real' education of her girls, commenting that 'some of them go to the day school three half days a week.'

Some of the children's comments from the lace schools tell a pitiful story of how their education was restricted by the need to make their livings and, of course, by the general attitude of the time that it did not pay to educate a girl.

Extract: village – Wilshampstead

Mary Pearce aged 10 – here two years. Hours from eight am to five pm: not longer. Learned sewing and reading at school before but not writing, summing or figures. (Spells one syllable words) Does not know what 'gay' or 'king' means, and does not know the queens name. Does not work at home. Has taken home 1s 8d to mother in a week for three collars!

Extract: village – Houghton Conquest

Dora Woodruff aged 11 – Can read, but not write or sum. Learned reading at school and goes on Sunday.

Jane Sorrell aged nine – Can read (short words) cannot tell what guard means and has never heard of a mountain.

Of course, it was generally believed that a woman should not bother her head with anything other than that strictly necessary to prepare herself for a life of drudgery, either in service or in her own home, raising children and making lace. No other future was envisaged for her, so of what use was learning?

Many children started at day schools, only to be taken away by their parents and sent instead to the lace schools, Marston Moretaine being no stranger to that practice. Even up until 1870 there were several lace schools still in existence in this village with up to 40 lacemakers attending, with no education being offered to them outside of lacemaking. A solution to this unfortunate situation was contrived when, in the December of 1873, Mr James Wood, the sub-Inspector of Factories, visited the Marston and Lidlington Lace Schools and attempted to persuade as many girls as possible to attend the National School as half-timers. He must have been quite persuasive, for the master at the National School, a Mr George Ferraby, later received a list of 37 'lacemaking girls' who were intending to become half-timers. To Mr Ferraby's delight, within a few days 33 of those enrolled, and his original expectations were exceeded when, in the next week, eight more arrived. However, the attendance of these new scholars left much to be desired, and in the February of the following year he reported that 'nearly all of the so-called half timers have left'. In April, when out of 41 only two or three were still in attendance, the local factory inspector went to work on this problem, and after re-visiting the lace schools the attendance rose once again, until 27 of the originals had returned.

Some lacemakers worked two collars a week, though not of this sort. These are possibly inspired by Lester's designs and are among many that sought to include natural elements of leaves and flowers within Bedford work (author's collection)

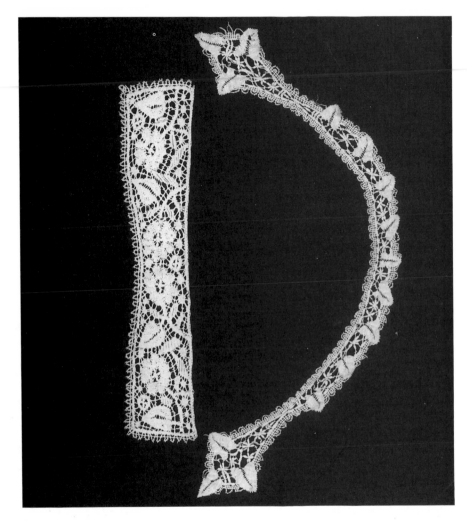

Attendance, however, was to continue to be a regular problem, the lacemaking girls being torn between the need to finish the lace set, and the need to attend school. During the period up to 1877 it became necessary to prosecute several of the lace schools for running a workshop without a licence to employ children, but the punishment was hardly severe enough to deter them from continuing the practice. Some of the difficulties may have been allayed when the Marston school board opened its premises at Upper Shelton, much nearer to home for a good half of its pupils, who by now also included boys, who half-timed between agricultural work and school. However, the mistress, a Miss Wells, was deeply concerned by how dull and backward the lacemaking girls seemed, and wrote in her report to the Board that the lace half-timers seemed to have no interest in their work and were not making any progress at their books. She was later forced to add that several other half-timers admitted to the Upper Shelton School were also extremely unruly.

When the 1876 Education Act was passed, many local authorities appointed attendance committees, and under the Amphill Union a Mr Fawcett of Flitton was appointed as the local school attendance officer for the area. When the Marston school board opened, he became responsible for attendance at the schools in Upper Shelton and Marston, but the attendance problem with half-timers was never satisfactorily resolved. Many areas of Bedfordshire refused to allow half-timing, possibly because of the difficulty of over-seeing school attendance, and it has to be said that although this practice continued in Marston Moretaine throughout many changes in education policy right up until 1903, it was never wholly acceptable.

However, as education gradually became accepted as the norm, regular school attendance increased and the lace schools fell into disuse. Very little information exists as to the actual dates on which they closed, but it is generally accepted that by 1880 full-time lace schools were no longer practising. Although they had ceased in their original form, and no longer

An example of Lester's ability to draw designs from nature and reproduce in lace the most unlikely things (by kind permission of the Trustees, the Cecil Higgins Art Gallery, Bedford)

threatened the future of full-time education, some of them continued in the evenings to teach lace and to provide an outlet for the lace produced at home.

One of Lester's concerns was the need for proper tuition in lacemaking to establish a more acceptable level of competence. He commented that he preferred the standard of work achieved by those lacemakers who had been taught at home. Many dealers were in agreement; Millward and Armstrong of Olney were not alone in making suggestions about the need to set a much higher standard of workmanship amongst the village lacemakers. This cry was to be echoed through successive generations, and in particular by those intent on bringing about a revival in the fortunes of the industry and those

Thomas Lester's Lace Shop in Bedford (by kind permission of the Trustees, the Cecil Higgins Art Gallery, Bedford)

who worked in it. However, successive attempts to produce some sort of skilled education in lacemaking either never got off the ground, or failed because the villagers clung to the outmoded methods that they knew. Thus it became progressively harder to introduce innovations in the style of the lace made, and the standard to which it was made.

Lester attempted to introduce some incentives in his own industry by rewarding especially good workers with a bobbin, several of which inscribed 'from Lesters' are still in existence. However, many smaller and less

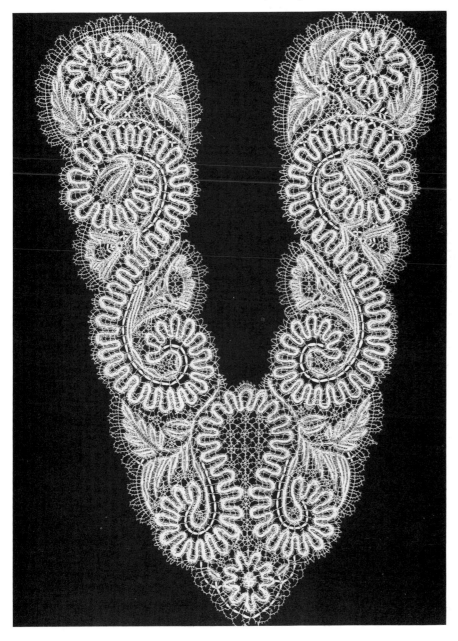

One of the finest Bedford lappett pieces, attributed to T. Lester of Bedford and the work of an exceptionally skilled lacemaker (by kind permission of the Trustees, the Cecil Higgins Art Gallery, Bedford)

particular dealers existed, of the type whose lace could be traded for groceries in a local store, and so there were still plenty of outlets for less than perfect lace, a factor which contributed to the general opinion that standards were declining as fast as the industry itself.

Despite Thomas Lester's flamboyant designs, the integration of techniques from Honiton and Malta, the growth of a lace style peculiar to Bedford and the apparently extraordinary numbers of lacemakers ready, willing and able to work, the decline in the trade could not be halted.

All over the Midlands valiant efforts were made to introduce new designs to attract the customer. The more elaborate styles of lace gave way to the introduction of Torchon designs, which were easy to interpret and quick to work, but still the industry continued its decline. In some ways, it must have seemed strange to local lacemakers that the traditional source of labour, i.e. children, were being encouraged into full-time education, and therefore denied to the industry. They also saw that the demand for lace had dropped off due to the introduction of machine lace, so little in the way of employment in the industry existed – yet there then came the attempts to revive the industry.

In 1891, during a visit to the Bedfordshire industry, A.S. Cole reported that the 'village industries were in a sad case, many of the patterns being

No less than the draft come to life. Lester's imagination knew no bounds, but he still needed the lacemaker to be able to interpret his designs (by kind permission of the Trustees, the Cecil Higgins Art Gallery, Bedford)

over fifty years old and now very inaccurate due to the practice of "pricking off" through the holes of a pattern too worn to work'. It would seem that design was in recession, for all the dealers were issuing were narrow edging patterns 'of inferior design'.

Coles's reports, throughout the periods of his travels through the major lacemaking counties of this country, all spelled out the same story: falling sales, failure to instruct in the advanced techniques of lacemaking, opportunities for employment outside the industry causing many to forsake the pillow, strong competition from the Nottinghamshire machine industry, and poor levels of design. In short, nationwide, the traditional lace industry was dying. He recommended trying to instigate a national standard of competence in lacemaking but, because of regional differences

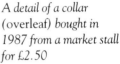

A detail of a collar (overleaf) bought in 1987 from a market stall for £2.50

Bedford lace collar bought for £2.50 in 1988. Lace is still seriously undervalued!

in techniques and marketing, this would have been extremely difficult to handle and, the Home Office, who commissioned the report into the failing trade, failed to act on any of his suggestions, preferring to allow those private individuals who chose to concern themselves with the problems of the industries to correct matters as best they could. The Lace Associations of the times then became the most common route through which lacemakers of the Midland industries marketed their work.

The North Buckinghamshire Lace Association has generally been viewed as the most businesslike of the many Associations set up for the purpose of supporting the flagging lace trade. It was instituted in 1897 and was, in fact, specifically re-organized into the North Bucks and Bedfordshire Association in order to include the work of the Bedford lacemakers. It boasted an impressive number of royal patrons and, in the early years of the twentieth century, its connections with the Belgian refugees of the First World War served to further its aims, which were to 'encourage the making of fine lace and to facilitate its sale direct from worker to purchaser securing for the worker an adequate return for skilled labour'. However, in common with many amateur businesses, it tended to under-sell the lacemakers' work.

By 1907 yet another committee had been formed in Bedfordshire, the Bedfordshire Lace Education Committee, which sought to continue education in lacemaking so that the craft might be preserved. Some areas of Northamptonshire had already experimented with education in traditional lacemaking, and the Bedford Committee hoped to revive the craft in this way. They were deeply reliant on the oldest lacemakers in the county for the Point Ground patterns of a previous era, for none but the coarser laces of the Bedford/Maltese style had been taught since 1870. The Committee were able to demonstrate that sales aplenty still existed for the fine Point Ground, but in 1924 the Lace Education Committee decided that commercial work should not be carried out at educational establishments. The result of this change in policy meant that actual sales in lace were curtailed, although a few schools continued to teach the skill until approximately 1930.

It is clear to see that given the trend of modern living, the adoption of a different way of life and mode of dress, that nothing any of our predecessors might have done could have prevented the demise of the industry. Furthermore, it is fairly easy to see that for the lacemaker, there was little or no possibility of advancing her case, neither financially nor in status from the little she earned at the pillow. Thankfully, enough of the craft was preserved by those involved in the dying years of the industry for us to have inherited the pleasure of the pillow with none of the pain.

It remains only for me to tell you where to go to see the collections held in local museums and galleries, and to hope that I will meet you, and see what you made of the patterns and stories of my home county.

PLACES TO GO

For details of opening times, please write or telephone before you visit.

The Cecil Higgins Art Gallery
Bedford
(Tel: 0234 211222)
Enquiries should be addressed to:
The Curator's Secretary
(Thomas Lester's Lace Reserve by special arrangement
Lace groups by arrangement)

County Museum
Temple Street
Aylesbury
(Tel: 0296 88849)

Cowper and Newton Museum
Market Square
Olney
Buckinghamshire
(Tel: 0234 711516)
Curator: Mrs Doreen Osborne
(Reserve on application)

Luton Museum
Wardown Park Road
Wardown Park
(Tel: 0582 36941)
Keeper of Textiles: Jill Draper

Liz Bartlett organizes tours of the lacemaking villages. For information, please telephone or write to the address given in the Suppliers section (p. 140–1).

BIBLIOGRAPHY

Buck, A.: *Thomas Lester, his Lace and the East Midlands Industry 1820–1905*, published by Ruth Bean, 1981

Brown, Dr O.F.: *Stony Stratford – The Town on the Road*, published by the Wolverton and District Archaeological Society, 1987

Hatley, V.A. (ed.): Northants Militia Lists 1777, Northants Record Society Vol. XXV

Hyde and Markham: *A History of Stony Stratford*

Markham, Sir Frank: *History of Milton Keynes and District*, volumes 1 and 2, White Crescent Press, 1973, 1975

Roundell, The Rev. H.: *Some account of the Town of Buckingham*, 1857, re-published by Bernard Cavalot in 1989*

Spencley, G.R.F.: *The Lace Associations: Philanthropic Movements to Preserve the Production of Hand-made Lace in Late Victorian and Edwardian England; Victorian Studies XVI, pp 433–52, 1973*

Wright, T.: *The Romance of the Lace Pillow*, Olney 1919, 1924, reprint 1971

Various articles collected by the Bedfordshire Historical Record Society and published in the Bedfordshire Magazine

* Note: always concerned with the history of the locality, Bernard Cavalot has been successful in finding and re-publishing several very interesting works written at the time that the lace industry was flourishing. He has found many references of great significance regarding the history of lace in Stony Stratford and is always willing to assist lacemakers, often being able to supply rare books which may be otherwise unobtainable. He can be contacted at: 10 York Road, Stony Stratford, Bucks, MK11 1BJ.

LACEMAKING GROUPS

Sherington Lace Group
8 Hillview
Sherington
Nr Olney
Bucks

Plantagenet Lacemakers
12 Creslow Court
Galley Hill
Stony Stratford
Bucks

Suppliers and sources of information

BOOK SUPPLIERS

UNITED KINGDOM
*The following are stockists of the
complete Batsford/Dryad Press
range:*

Avon
Bridge Bookshop
7 Bridge Street
Bath BA2 4AS

Waterstone & Co.
4–5 Milsom Street
Bath BA1 1DA

Bedfordshire
Arthur Sells
Lane Cove
49 Pedley Lane
Clifton
Shefford SG17 5QT

Berkshire
Loricraft
4 Big Lane
Lambourn

West End Lace Supplies
Ravensworth Court Road
Mortimer West End
Reading RG7 3UD

Buckinghamshire
J. S. Sear Lacecraft Supplies
8 Hillview
Sheringham MK16 9NY

Cambridgeshire
Dillons the Bookstore
Sidney Street
Cambridge

Cheshire
Lyn Turner
Church Meadow Crafts
15 Carisbrook Drive
Winsford CW7 1LN

Cornwall
Creative Books
22A River Street
Truro TR1 2SJ

Devon
Creative Crafts & Needlework
18 High Street
Totnes TQ9 5NP

Honiton Lace Shop
44 High Street
Honiton EX14 8PJ

Dorset
F. Herring & Sons
High West Street
Dorchester DT1 1UP

Tim Parker (mail order)
124 Corhampton Road
Boscombe East
Bournemouth BH6 5NL

Durham
Lacemaid
6, 10 & 15 Stoneybeck
Bishop Middleham DL17 9BL

Gloucestershire
Southgate Handicrafts
68 Southgate Street
Gloucester GL1 1TX

Waterstone & Co.
89–90 The Promenade
Cheltenham GL50 1NB

Hampshire
Creative Crafts
11 The Square
Winchester SO23 9ES

Doreen Gill
14 Barnfield Road
Petersfield GU31 4DR

Larkfield Crafts
4 Island Cottages
Mapledurwell
Basingstoke RG23 2LU

Needlestyle
24–26 West Street
Alresford

Ruskins
27 Bell Street
Romsey

Isle of Wight
Busy Bobbins
Unit 7
Scarrots Lane
Newport PO30 1JD

Kent
The Handicraft Shop
47 Northgate
Canterbury CT1 1BE

Hatchards
The Great Hall
Mount Pleasant Road
Tunbridge Wells

London
W. & G. Foyles Ltd
113–119 Charing Cross Road
WC2H 0EB

Hatchards
187 Piccadilly W1V 9DA

Middlesex
Redburn Crafts
Squires Garden Centre
Halliford Road
Upper Halliford
Shepperton TW17 8RU

Norfolk
Alby Lace Museum
Cromer Road
Alby
Norwich NR11 7QE

Jane's Pincushions
Taverham Craft Unit 4
Taverham Nursery Centre
Fir Covert Road
Taverham
Norwich NR8 6HT

Waterstone & Co.
30 London Street
Norwich NR2 1LD

Northamptonshire
Denis Hornsby
149 High Street
Burton Latimer
Kettering NN15 5RL

Somerset
Bridge Bookshop
62 Bridge Street
Taunton TA1 1UD

Staffordshire
J. & J. Ford
October Hill
65 Upper Way
Upper Longdon
Rugeley WS16 1QB

Sussex
Waterstone & Company Ltd
120 Terminus Road
Eastbourne

Warwickshire
Christine & David Springett
21 Hillmorton Road
Rugby CV22 6DF

Wiltshire
Everyman Bookshop
5 Bridge Street
Salisbury SP1 2ND

North Yorkshire
Craft Basics
9 Gillygate
York

Shireburn Lace
Finkel Court
Finkel Hill
Sherburn in Elmet
LS25 6EB

Valley House Craft Studios
Ruston
Scarborough YO13 9QE

West Midlands
Needlewoman
Needles Alley
off New Street
Birmingham

West Yorkshire
Sebalace
Waterloo Mill
Howden Road
Silsden BD20 0HA

George White Lacemaking
  Supplies
40 Heath Drive
Boston Spa LS23 6PB

Jo Firth
58 Kent Crescent
Lowtown
Pudsey
Leeds LS28 9EB

WALES
Bryncraft Bobbins (mail order)
B. J. Phillips
Pantglas
Cellan
Lampeter
Dyfed SA48 BJD

SCOTLAND
Embroidery Shop
51 Willian Street
Edinburgh
Lothian EH3 7LW

Waterstone & Co.
236 Union Street
Aberdeen AB1 1TN

EQUIPMENT SUPPLIERS

UNITED KINGDOM
Alby Lace Museum
Cromer Road
Alby
Norwich
Norfolk NR11 7QE

Busy Bobbins
Unit 7
Scarrots Lane
Newport
IOW
PO30 1JD

Chosen Crafts Centre
46 Winchcombe Street
Cheltenham
Glos GL52 2ND

Jo Firth
Lace Marketing & Needlecraft
  Supplies
58 Kent Crescent
Lowtown
Pudsey
W Yorks LS28 9EB

J. & J. Ford
October Hill
Upper Way
Upper Longdon
Rugeley
Staffs WS15 1QB

R. Gravestock
Highwood
Crews Hill
Alfrick
Worcs WR6 5HF

The Handicraft Shop
47 Northgate
Canterbury
Kent CT1 1BE

Frank Herring & Sons
27 High West Street
Dorchester
Dorset DT1 1UP

Honiton Lace Shop
44 High Street
Honiton
Devon

Denis Hornsby
149 High Street
Burton Latimer
Kettering
Northants NN15 5RL
    also at:
25 Manwood Avenue
Canterbury
Kent CT2 7AH

Frances Iles
73 High Street
Rochester
Kent ME1 1LX

Jane's Pincushions
Unit 4
Taverham Crafts
Taverham Nursery Centre
Fir Covert Road
Taverham
Norwich NR8 6HT

Loricraft
4 Big Lane
Lambourn
Berkshire

Iris Martin
1 Farthing Cottage
Clickers Yard
Olney
Bucks
(*also antique bobbins*)

Needlestyle
5 The Woolmead
Farnham
Surrey GU9 7TX

Needlestyle
24–26 West Street
Alresford
Hants

Needlework
Ann Bartleet
Bucklers Farm
Coggeshall
Essex CO6 1SB

Needle and Thread
80 High Street
Horsell
Woking
Surrey GU21 4SZ

The Needlewoman
21 Needles Alley
off New Street
Birmingham B2 5AE

T. Parker
124 Corhampton Road
Boscombe East
Bournemouth
Dorset BH6 5NZ

Jane Playford
North Lodge
Church Close
West Runton
Norfolk NR27 9QY

Redburn Crafts
Squires Garden Centre
Halliford Road
Upper Halliford
Shepperton
Middx TW17 8RU

Christine Riley
53 Barclay Street
Stonehaven
Kincardineshire
Scotland

Peter & Beverley Scarlett
Strupak
Hill Head
Cold Wells
Ellon
Grampian
Scotland

Ken & Pat Schultz
134 Wisbech Road
Thornley
Peterborough

J. S. Sears
Lacecraft Supplies
8 Hillview
Sherington
Bucks MK16 9NY

Sebalace
Waterloo Mills
Howden Road
Silsden
W Yorks BD2 0NA

A. Sells
49 Pedley Lane
Clifton
Shefford
Beds

Shireburn Lace
Finkle Court
Finkle Hill
Sherburn in Elmet
N Yorks LS25 6EB

SMP
4 Garners Close
Chalfont St Peter
Bucks SL9 0HB

Southern Handicrafts
20 Kensington Gardens
Brighton
Sussex BN1 4AC

Spangles
Carole Morris
Cashburn Lace
Burwell
Cambs CB5 0ED

Stitchery
Finkle Street
Richmond
N Yorks

Stitches
Dovehouse Shopping Parade
Warwick Road
Olton
Solihull
W Midlands

Teazle Embroideries
35 Boothferry Road
Hull
N Humberside

Lynn Turner
Church Meadow Crafts
15 Carisbrooke Drive
Winsford
Cheshire CW7 1LN

Valley House Craft Studios
Ruston
Scarborough
N Yorks

George Walker
The Corner Shop
Rickinghall
Diss
Norfolk

West End Lace Supplies
Ravensworth Court Road
Mortimer West End
Reading
Berks RG7 3UD

George White Lacemakers'
    Supplies
40 Heath Drive
Boston Spa
W Yorks L23 6PB

Bobbins
A. R. Arches
The Poplars
Shetland
near Stowmarket
Suffolk IP14 3DE

Liz Bartlett
Bartlett, Caesar and Partners
12 Creslow Court
Stony Stratford
Milton Keynes MK11 1NN
(tel. 0908 263301)

Bartlett, Caesar and Partners
The Glen
Shorefield Road
Downton
Lymington
Hants SO41 0LH
(tel. 0590 644854)

T. Brown
Temple Lane Cottage
Littledean
Cinderford
Glos

Bryncraft Bobbins
B. J. Phillips
Pantglas
Cellan
Lampeter
Dyfed SA48 BJD

Chrisken Bobbins
26 Cedar Drive
Kingsclere
Bucks RG15 8TD

Malcolm J. Fielding
2 Northern Terrace
Moss Lane
Silverdale
Lancs LA5 0ST

Richard Gravestock
Highwood
Crews Hill
Alfrick
Worcs WR6 5HF

Larkfield Crafts
Hilary Ricketts
4 Island Cottages
Mapledurwell
Basingstoke
Hants RG25 2LU

Loricraft
4 Big Lane
Lambourn
Berkshire

T. Parker
124 Corhampton Road
Boscombe East
Bournemouth
Dorset BH6 5NZ

D. H. Shaw
47 Lamor Crescent
Thrushcroft
Rotherham
S Yorks S66 9QD

Sizelands
1 Highfield Road
Winslow
Bucks MK10 3QU

Christine & David Springett
21 Hillmorton Road
Rugby
War CV22 5DF

Richard Viney
Unit 7
Port Royal Street
Southsea
Hants PO5 3UD

West End Lace Suppliers
Ravensworth Court Road
Mortimer West End
Reading
Berks RG7 3UD

Lace pillows
Newnham Lace Equipment
15 Marlowe Close
Basingstoke
Hants RG24 9DD

Liz Bartlett
Bartlett, Caesar and Partners
12 Creslow Court
Stony Stratford
Milton Keynes MK11 1NN
(tel. 0908 263301)

Bartlett, Caesar and Partners
The Glen
Shorefield Road
Downton
Lymington
Hants SO41 0LH

Silk embroidery and lace thread
E. & J. Piper
Silverlea
Flax Lane
Glemsford
Suffolk CO10 7RS

Silk weaving yarn
Hilary Chetwynd
Kipping Cottage
Cheriton
Alresford
Hants SO24 0PW

Frames and mounts
Doreen Campbell
Highcliff
Bremilham Road
Malmesbury
Wilts SN16 0DQ

**Matt coloured transparent
   adhesive film**
Heffers Graphic Shop
26 King Street
Cambridge CB1 1LN

**Linen by the metre (yard) and
   made up articles of church
   linen**
Mary Collins
Church Furnishings
St Andrews Hall
Humber Doucy Lane
Ipswich
Suffolk IP4 3BP

Hayes & Finch
Head Office & Factory
Hanson Road
Aintree
Liverpool L9 9BP

**UNITED STATES OF
   AMERICA**
Arbor House
22 Arbor Lane
Roslyn Hights
NY 11577

Baltazor Inc.
3262 Severn Avenue
Metairie
LA 7002

Beggars' Lace
P.O. Box 17263
Denver
Colo 80217

Berga Ullman Inc.
P.O. Box 918
North Adams
MA 01247

Frederick J. Fawcett
129 South Street
Boston
MA 02130

Frivolité
15526 Densmore N.
Seattle
WA 98113

Happy Hands
3007 S. W. Marshall
Pendleton
Oreg 97180

International Old Lacers
P.O. Box 1029
Westminster
Colo 80030

Lace Place de Belgique
800 S. W. 17th Street
Boca Raton
FL 33432

Lacis
2150 Stuart Street
Berkeley
CA 9470

Robin's Bobbins
RTL Box 1736
Mineral Bluff
GA 30559

Robin and Russ
Handweavers
533 North Adams Street
McMinnvills
Oreg 97128

Some Place
2990 Adline Street
Berkeley
CA 94703

Osma G. Todd Studio
319 Mendoza Avenue
Coral Gables
FL 33134

The Unique and Art Lace
   Cleaners
5926 Delman Boulevard
St Louis
MO 63112

Van Scriver Bobbin Lace
130 Cascadilla Park
Ithaca
NY 14850

The World in Stitches
82 South Street
Milford
N.H. 03055

AUSTRALIA

Australian Lace magazine
P.O. Box 1291
Toowong
Queensland 4066

Dentelles Lace Supplies
c/o Betty Franks
39 Lang Terrace
Northgate 4013
Brisbane
Queensland

The Lacemaker
94 Fordham Avenue
Hartwell
Victoria 3124

Spindle and Loom
Arcade 83
Longueville Road
Lane Cove
NSW 2066

Tulis Crafts
201 Avoca Street
Randwick
NSW 2031

BELGIUM

't Handwerkhuisje
Katelijnestraat 23
8000 Bruges

Kantcentrum
Balstraat 14
8000 Bruges

Manufacture Belge de Dentelle
6 Galerie de la Reine
Galeries Royales St Hubert
1000 Bruxelles

Orchidée
Mariastraat 18
8000 Bruges

Ann Thys
't Apostelientje
Balstraat 11
8000 Bruges

FRANCE

Centre d'Initiations à la
    Dentelle du Puy
2 Rue Duguesclin
43000 Le Puy en Velay

A L'Econome
Anne-Marie Deydier
Ecole de Dentelle aux Fuseaux
10 rue Paul Chenavard
69001 Lyon

Rougier and Plé
13–15 bd des Filles de Calvaire
75003 Paris

WEST GERMANY

Der Fenster Laden
Berliner Str. 8
D 6483 Bad Soden
Salmünster

P.P. Hempel
Ortolanweg 34
1000 Berlin 47

Heikona De Ruijter
Kleoppelgrosshandel
Langer Steinweg 38
D4933 Blomberg

HOLLAND

Blokker's Boektiek
Bronsteeweg 4/4a
2101 AC Heemstede

Theo Brejaat
Postbus 5199
3008 AD Rotterdam

Magazijn *De Vlijt*
Lijnmarkt 48, Utrecht

SWITZERLAND

Fadehax, Inh. Irene Solca
4105 Biel-Benken, Basel

NEW ZEALAND

Peter McLeavey
P.O. Box 69.007
Auckland 8

SOURCES OF INFORMATION

UNITED KINGDOM

The Lace Guild
The Hollies
53 Audnam, Stourbridge
West Midlands DY8 4AE

The Lacemakers' Circle
49 Wardwick
Derby DE1 1HY

The Lace Society
Linwood
Stratford Road
Oversley, Alcester
War BY9 6PG

The British College of Lace
21 Hillmorton Road
Rugby
War CV22 5DF

The English Lace School
Oak House
Church Stile
Woodbury, Nr Exeter
Devon

United Kingdom Director of
    International Old Lacers
S. Hurst
4 Dollius Road
London N3 1RG

Ring of Tatters
Mrs C. Appleton
Nonesuch
5 Ryeland Road
Ellerby, Saltbury by Sea
Cleveland TS13 5LP

U.S.A

International Old Lacers
Gunvor Jorgensen (Pres.)
366 Bradley Avenue
Northvale, NJ 076647

INDEX